# A Simple Guide to Matthew

# A Simple Guide to Matthew

Paul J. McCarren, SJ

A SHEED & WARD BOOK

ROWMAN & LITTLEFIELD PUBLISHERS, INC.
Lanham • Boulder • New York • Toronto • Plymouth, UK

A Sheed & Ward Book

Published by Rowman & Littlefield Publishers, Inc.
A wholly owned subsidiary of The Rowman & Littlefield Publishing Group, Inc.
4501 Forbes Boulevard, Suite 200, Lanham, Maryland 20706
www.rowman.com

10 Thornbury Road, Plymouth PL6 7PY, United Kingdom

British Library Cataloguing in Publication Information Available

**Library of Congress Cataloging-in-Publication Data**

McCarren, Paul J., 1943–
A simple guide to Matthew / Paul J. Mccarren.
p. cm.
Includes index.
ISBN 978-1-4422-1887-1 (cloth : alk. paper)—ISBN 978-1-4422-1888-8 (pbk. : alk. paper)—ISBN 978-1-4422-1889-5 (electronic)
1. Bible. N.T. Matthew—Commentaries. I. Title.
BS2575.53.M423 2013
226.2'077—dc23
2012031922

Printed in the United States of America

# Contents

# Introduction: Why I Needed a Simple Guide to the Gospels

It took me a long time to hear what the Gospels say. Luckily, I spent much of that time with the Jesuits, an organization that is patient with slow learners. Like all the other religious orders in the Catholic Church, the Jesuits attempt to respond to Jesus' command in the Gospels to spread the Good News. So Jesuits are required to take time learning what's proclaimed in the Good News. One method used in this learning process is the Spiritual Exercises of Ignatius Loyola. Most of those exercises are contemplations of Gospel scenes that are undertaken with the help of a director, just as physical exercises are often done with the help of a trainer. Jesuits go through these exercises at least twice. I did the Spiritual Exercises as a Jesuit novice; but when I did them again years later, I was shocked to discover I had no idea what I was doing.

The shock hit me late one afternoon as I read to my director a description of how the exercises had gone that day. As I read, he began to cough and clear his throat. He reached for a tissue and said, "Sorry; please excuse me. I've sometimes cried while listening to a write-up, but I've never laughed so hard." My look must have said, "What's so funny?" So he asked me to listen to what I'd been writing. After he read from notes he'd taken on my write-ups, he said, "Notice how you're picturing Jesus." I'd been imagining Jesus acting as a stern teacher who could barely control his impatience with people's slowness to understand his message. Over and over in my prayers I had seen Jesus as a man who was quick to find fault with the mistakes made by his followers. After asking me to notice that this image wasn't very appealing, my director reminded me that the Gospels describe someone quite different from the Jesus I'd imagined. They tell us, for instance, that many people found Jesus immensely attractive. Some of them even dropped everything to follow him. I had missed this simple fact. How was that possible?

At some point in my life I had slipped into the assumption that, because the Gospels describe a God who is infinite, it must be infinitely difficult to relate to him. The logic of that assumption seemed as obvious as the fact that because the theories of modern physics are extremely complex, physics is extremely difficult to get your mind around. But the Gospels aren't complex theoretical reflections on mysterious truths—and they can't be understood as such. They are four descriptions of how Jesus struggled to share his love of God with others, and how his struggle succeeded. The Gospel writers relate this success to us as simple Good News that Jesus invited others to enjoy and spread.

With the help of my retreat director, I stopped looking for hidden lessons in the Gospel narratives. When I began to reread the Gospels without the prejudice of my assumptions, it became clear that, despite many differences in the four texts, each evangelist's narrative zeroed in on the same thing: Jesus' passionate drive to teach by his words and his actions. Biblical scholars have pointed out that we don't know precisely how the Gospel texts reached the form in which they are now presented in the Bible. The Gospel of Luke glances at this fact when it begins with the note that accounts (yes, he says "accounts") had been handed down to the evangelist's generation by those who had witnessed Jesus' ministry [Lk.1:2]. Then the evangelist promises to organize this material so that the reader might come to "realize the certainty of the teachings" [Lk.1:4]. All the Gospel authors (or, if you like, all the editors and copyists who arranged the work of the original authors into the various manuscripts from which our modern Bibles are translated) seem to share this purpose: to make it plain that Jesus taught about God's determination to bring his work of creation to glorious fulfillment in us, his children.

Years ago on retreat, when my director nudged me to take a careful look at precisely what the Gospels say, I began to see them as attempts to let readers hear what Jesus struggled to teach his first disciples to hear: good news. With my director's encouragement to note the simple facts and details set down by the evangelists, I began to feel that even someone as benighted as myself could begin to take in the Gospel's simple message.

## WHY A SIMPLE GUIDE TO THE GOSPELS MIGHT HELP YOU

When I look back on my difficulty in noticing Jesus' simple proclamation of the Good News, I take comfort in the fact that my denseness isn't unique. For example, when Mark describes Jesus visiting Nazareth, his old neighbors are said to be so astonished by his teaching that they couldn't believe it. They ask, "Where did this man get all this?" [Mk.6:2]. What they heard seemed too good to be true, so they resolved the tension they felt between surprise and suspicion by choosing to be annoyed: "They took offense at him" [Mk.6:3]. Mark and the other evangelists relate such moments of rejection as dead ends—moments when the story they're telling comes to a temporary halt. In other scenes, however, doubt and astonishment don't end with a rejection of the Good News but lead to an awareness of its power to move the heart. For example, Luke describes the disciples' first response to seeing Jesus after his resurrection as a mix of bafflement and glee: "They were still incredulous for joy and were amazed" [Lk.24:41]. Here, the disciples' delight is said to be as real as their disbelief. A sense of befuddlement ("How can this be?") grips them even as they're filled with joy. One feeling doesn't cancel the other. Luke is telling us that doubts and suspicions needn't overwhelm us with dismay even when they're striking us with full force. What good news!

If you, like me (and like many disciples before us), have been confused by parts of the Gospel narratives, you too might benefit from some simple comments about each scene and event—such as my director's comment about the people who found Jesus fascinating. And you, like me, might be helped by noting that all of Jesus' followers had to grapple with his simple message before they could accept it. For instance, when the Gospel of Mark describes events after the resurrection, it portrays Jesus taking many disciples to task for their stubbornness: "He appeared to them and rebuked them for their unbelief and hardness of heart because they had not believed those who saw him after he had been raised" [Mk.16:14]. Recall, however, what Jesus says next to these slow learners: "He said to them, 'Go into the whole world and proclaim the Gospel to every creature'" [Mk.16:15]. Here Jesus entrusts the announcement of the Gospel—the Good News—to the very individuals who, when they first heard reports of the resurrection, couldn't believe them. It's natural to assume that, as these first disciples headed off to fulfill their commission to proclaim the Good News, they needed to review with one another what they thought the Good News was. They would have asked one another such questions as, "What was it he said that time we were caught in the storm; and what did we say in response?" As they recalled their various experiences of what Jesus had said and done, they would have helped one another review the recent past until they began to see a clear and communicable message—a message that others could grasp as Good News. In turn, those who heard this message began to write accounts of what they heard so still others could hear about Jesus and his struggle to proclaim God's truth as Good News. Each gospel proclaims this Good News, but each one proclaims it in a slightly different way.

## HOW IS MATTHEW'S GOSPEL DIFFERENT?

Trust: Matthew's Gospel may have been addressed to fellow Jews who, after the Romans destroyed Jerusalem and its Temple in 70 C.E., were unsure how to express their faith. This Gospel describes Jesus as a teacher who speaks to people filled with doubts about God's ability to fulfill the promises he made to Abraham and his descendants. In Matthew, Jesus doesn't hesitate to address the challenge people face: choose to trust that God can and will bring you to the glory of his kingdom, or presume that your fate is controlled by nothing more than the fickle unfolding of earthly events. We hear Jesus console believers with the assurance that, even when facing misfortune, they can put themselves wholeheartedly into God's care.

Scripture: The most casual reader of Matthew's Gospel will note that the author assumes his readers know about Jewish beliefs and practices. (Scripture scholars generally agree that the author of this Gospel—whom we call Matthew, though his identity is uncertain—was a Jew writing for Jews who knew the ancient Hebrew scriptures.) Matthew portrays Jesus delighting in the promises that animate these scriptures—telling his disciples they should expect to see the words of scripture fulfilled in someone who believes those words. Jesus, of course, is the perfect example of the true believer—who asks his disciples to follow his example.

Sayings: In this Gospel, we find Jesus teaching with many short sayings—more sayings than in the other Gospels. (John's Gospel has long addresses, but fewer pithy sayings.) Matthew describes Jesus sharing these concise teachings to help hearers realize that the stories, poems, and reflections that make up the ancient scriptures pose a simple question: do you want to accept the intimate relationship that God offers in the Covenant?

Discourses: Most of the sayings recorded by Matthew are found in sections referred to by scholars as "Discourses." The most famous of these is popularly known as the Sermon on the Mount [Mt.5–7]. It might be more accurate to picture that event as the first of several lively seminars, not speeches, in which Jesus prods his listeners to reconsider their assumptions about God. You, the reader, are a member of each seminar. Because you're not simply part of a crowd following a closely reasoned speech, you can feel free to pause at any time to reflect on a question or review what's been said.

As we read Matthew's Gospel, we're invited by the evangelist to listen to Jesus reassure his disciples that God's promises, repeated over and over in the ancient scriptures, are trustworthy. Watch, says Jesus, as I entrust myself to the God who has made these promises; taste and see how gracious, loving, and merciful he is; then, follow me.

For other subjects stressed in Matthew's Gospel, see the index.

## A TRANSLATION CHALLENGE

The Gospels were written in Greek. Many Gospel translations, including those in lectionaries used for formal church services, have been prepared by commissions of scholars. These translations not only render into English the words of the Greek text but also retain the original rhetorical phrasings. Because ancient Greek phrasing is different from modern English expression, a strictly literal translation is often hard to follow. The simplicity of an evangelist's message can escape us when a translation retains its original (and unfamiliar) turns of phrase.

When preachers begin a homily, they often rephrase whatever text has just been proclaimed. They want to make sure we know what the text actually says before they begin to comment on it. So, after a reading, they're likely to say something like, "Did you notice what the evangelist was saying there? Let me put it another way, just so we don't miss his point." Like a preacher's careful rephrasing of a text, my translation of Matthew's Gospel in this simple guide spells out anything that might be muddled or missed in a strictly literal translation of the original Greek words and phrases. The translation also includes occasional explanatory remarks that, in other translations, are relegated to footnotes or the accompanying commentary. I've put such explanations within the passages to let you keep reading Matthew's Good News without having to stop to look up unfamiliar references.

## ACKNOWLEDGMENTS

My comments after each section of my translation are derived from the study of many scripture commentaries. I am indebted in particular to the richness of the notes and commentary by Daniel J. Harrington, SJ, published in the Sacra Pagina series of studies of the New Testament, and to the wealth of information in the notes and commentary of W. F. Albright and C. S. Mann, published as part of the Anchor Bible.

Many people encouraged me during the writing of the manuscript and helped me with comments on it. Thank you to Bridget Leonard, who worked long and hard as a literary agent for this work, and to Carole Sargent for her guidance at Georgetown University's Office of Scholarly and Literary Publication. And thank you to the parishioners at the parishes where I worked—especially to Dorothy Davis, Agnes Williams, Jayne Ikard, and Tom and Mary Biddle. Other helpful comments came from my sister, Morgan, and from my friends Jean Reynolds and Alan Wynroth. I am grateful to my provincial superior of the Maryland Province of the Jesuits, who allowed me time to write this book, and to all my supportive Jesuit companions, especially James P. M. Walsh, SJ.

# ONE

# The Ancestry and Birth of Jesus

## JESUS' ANCESTORS [MT.1:1–17]

¹ *This is a record of the ancestry of Jesus, the Christ, son of David, son of Abraham.* ² *Abraham: father of Isaac. Isaac: father of Jacob. Jacob: father of Judah and his brothers.* ³ *Judah: father of Perez and Zerah; mother: Tamar. Perez: father of Hezron. Hezron: father of Aram.* ⁴ *Aram: father of Aminadab. Aminadab: father of Nahshon. Nahshon: father of Salmon.* ⁵ *Salmon: father of Boaz; mother: Rahab. Boaz: father of Obed; mother: Ruth. Obed: father of Jesse.* ⁶ *Jesse: father of David, the king.*

*David: father of Solomon; mother: the wife of Uriah.* ⁷ *Solomon: father of Rehoboam. Rehoboam: father of Abijah. Abijah: father of Asaph.* ⁸ *Asaph: father of Jehoshaphat. Jehoshaphat: father of Joram. Joram: father of Uzziah.* ⁹ *Uzziah: father of Jotham. Jotham: father of Ahaz. Ahaz: father of Hezekiah.* ¹⁰ *Hezekiah: father of Manasseh. Manasseh: father of Amos. Amos: father of Josiah.* ¹¹ *Josiah: father of Jechoniah and his brothers at the time of the Babylonian exile.*

¹² *After the exile into Babylon, Jechoniah: father of Shealtiel. Shealtiel: father of Zerubbabel.* ¹³ *Zerubbabel: father of Abiud. Abiud: father of Eliakim. Eliakim: father of Azor.* ¹⁴ *Azor: father of Zadok. Zadok: father of Achim. Achim: father of Eliud.* ¹⁵ *Eliud: father of Eleazar. Eleazar: father of Matthan. Matthan: father of Jacob.* ¹⁶ *Jacob: father of Joseph. Joseph was the husband of Mary, from whom was born Jesus, the one who is called "the Christ."*

*[17]* *Generations from Abraham to David: fourteen. Generations from David to the exile in Babylon: fourteen. Generations from the Babylonian exile to the Christ: fourteen.*

The first sentence of this Gospel emphasizes three things. First, Jesus is the Christ—that is, the one "anointed" or particularly chosen by God for a special purpose. (The Greek for the "Anointed One" is translated "the Christ." In Hebrew, it's "Messiah.") Second, it says Jesus is in the line of David, and, third, he's a child of Abraham—two claims supported by a genealogy. But the genealogy doesn't give a simple list of who begat whom. Matthew breaks the simple father-to-son pattern of the genealogy with the mention of four women. And, at the end, he highlights the fact that he's set down three lists of fourteen—although the last one amounts to thirteen. What's going on here?

First, notice who the women are. In the Bible, Tamar [v.3] is portrayed using subterfuge to make Judah fulfill a promise of marriage (see Gen.38). Rahab [v.5] is described as a Gentile prostitute who believed that the God who had made a Covenant with the people of Israel was the true and only God (see Jos.2). Ruth [v.5] is presented as a Moabite, not an Israelite, who also believed in the God of the Covenant (see the Book of Ruth). Matthew doesn't mention Bathsheba's name. But, referring to her as Uriah's wife [v.6], he reminds us that the Second Book of Samuel describes David conceiving a child with her in an act of adultery (see 2 Sm.11). Without a note from the author explaining his decision to refer to these women, we're left to our natural reactions—one of which might be: "How surprisingly God works out his special purpose for his Chosen One."

Second, though everyone who has trouble balancing a checkbook can take comfort from Matthew's mistake in addition, a simple fact can't be obscured by his miscount. The simple fact is, he's listed many generations. Or, to put it another way, God certainly takes time to unfold his divine plan. And nothing—not even a lengthy exile for his people—seems able to deter God from fulfilling that plan.

Matthew's genealogy doesn't give us an objective look at the forces of history. Nor does it give Jesus an impressive human pedigree—especially with the dignity of earthly royalty looking less than sterling as it's embodied by David. The genealogy is a lesson in how God is patiently at work in human affairs in ways that puzzle us. Does that sound like Good News?

## JESUS IS BORN [MT.1:18–25]

*18 The birth of Jesus, the Christ, happened like this. His mother, Mary, was engaged to Joseph. But before they came together, she was found pregnant—of the Holy Spirit. 19 Because her husband, Joseph, was righteous, he didn't want to disgrace her. He decided to divorce her secretly. 20 This is what he was planning when, imagine, an angel of the Lord appeared to him in a dream and said, "Joseph, son of David, don't be afraid to take Mary as your wife. Her child was conceived from the Holy Spirit. 21 She'll bear a son. You'll name him, 'Jesus'—[a shortened form of 'Joshua,' which was understood to mean 'God helps' or 'God saves']—because he will save his people from their sins." 22 All this showed how fully the Lord spoke the truth through the prophet [Isaiah]: 23 "Look! The virgin will be pregnant. She'll bear a son. They'll name him 'Emmanuel.'" Emmanuel means "God is with us." 24 Joseph got up and did what the angel of the Lord told him—he took her as his wife. 25 But he didn't know her sexually until she bore a son. He named him Jesus.*

The description of Mary's pregnancy fits into the pattern of surprising events of which Matthew reminded us in the genealogy. He emphasizes this with his note that the pregnancy was accomplished by God's Spirit [v.18]. Joseph's first reaction, on the other hand, isn't at all surprising. He's described confronting a practical problem with a sensible decision. In so doing, of course, he doesn't take the view suggested by the genealogy: God works in marvelous and unpredictable ways [v.19]. But then we hear he was told to accept the possibility that God was at work. He was asked to cooperate in God's plan to turn people away from selfishness—away from sin [vv.20–21].

Matthew then asks us to reflect on the truth the angel asked Joseph to acknowledge. It's the truth, told over and over in scripture, that God intends to complete the work of creation, and that he will do so in surprising ways. Matthew cites a story from the Book of Isaiah (see Is.7:10–14) about a king who refused to act on Isaiah's instruction to turn to God to save his kingdom. Despite the king's unwillingness to cry out to God for care and reassurance, God nonetheless gave a sign of his care by promising that a young woman would have a son who would assure the kingdom that "God is with us" [vv.22–23]. With this analogy, Matthew is confronting us with the same question Isaiah put to the king: "Do you believe God can and will fulfill his plan?"

We then hear that, unlike the king in Isaiah's story, Joseph readily accepted God's plan as it was announced to him [v.24]. Matthew adds that, although Joseph had no part in conceiving Jesus, he took full responsibility for him as his son—just as the angel said he should when Joseph was asked to name the child Jesus [v.25].

# TWO
## Jesus' Infancy

VISITORS FROM THE EAST [MT.2:1–12]

*¹ When Jesus was born in Bethlehem of Judea, Herod was king in Jerusalem. Imagine, magi from the east arrived in Jerusalem. ² They asked, "Where is the newborn who is king of the Jews? We saw his star rise, and we've come to pay him homage." ³ When they heard this, Herod and all Jerusalem were unsettled. ⁴ Herod called together all the chief priests and scribes of the people and asked them where the Christ would be born. ⁵ "In Bethlehem of Judea," they said. "A prophet wrote: ⁶ 'And you, Bethlehem in Judah, are hardly the least of Judah's rulers. For a ruler will come from you [see Mi.5:1]. He will shepherd my people Israel'" [see 2 Sm.5:2]. ⁷ Herod called in the magi secretly and asked the time of the star's rising. ⁸ Then he sent them to Bethlehem: "Go find whatever you can about this child. Then tell me what you find so I may pay him homage too." ⁹ They listened to the king, left, and, imagine, the star they'd seen in the east went before them until it stopped over the place of the child. ¹⁰ Their delight in seeing the star couldn't be contained. ¹¹ They arrived at the dwelling. They saw his mother, Mary. They bent down and did homage to him. They opened treasures for him: gold, frankincense, and myrrh. ¹² A dream warned them not to go back to Herod. They went home another way.*

―❧―

Matthew doesn't tell us the nationality, profession, or number of the magi. But he does say they came from the east and knew little about the "newborn king," yet wanted to offer him homage [vv.1–2]. The confusion Matthew describes in Herod and the people of Jerusalem seems reasonable: since Herod is the king, how can there be a new king? But when we hear that Herod's confusion was dispelled by information from Jewish teachers, no one is depicted receiving this as good news. The teachers would know scripture's many descriptions of God's promise to provide direction for his people—even from such unlikely places as Bethlehem. But Matthew doesn't say they spoke to Herod about God's promise. Instead, we hear them say little more than "Look in Bethlehem" [vv.3–6].

As described by Matthew, Herod's question to the magi about the star sounds like banter before getting to his real interest: "Find me that child!" According to Matthew, Herod's desire to pay homage wasn't so great that he joined the magi; he was willing to wait for a report [vv.7–8]. We hear that the magi were thrilled by the reappearance of the star, and that they fulfilled their goal by expressing their reverence with gestures and gifts [vv.9–11]. Matthew tells us that the magi—like Joseph, who was moved by God's message in a dream to trust other instincts than his own (see 1:24)—accepted the guidance of a dream, and then went home [v.12].

## JESUS' FAMILY FLEES; HEROD TYRANNIZES; THE FAMILY RETURNS [MT.2:13–23]

*13 After the magi left, imagine, an angel of the Lord appeared to Joseph in a dream and said, "Get up. Flee with the child and his mother to Egypt. Stay there till I tell you. Herod's going to try to find and kill him." 14 That very night, he got up, took the child and his mother, and left for Egypt. 15 He stayed there until Herod died. How fully the prophet [Hosea] spoke the Lord's truth when he said, "Out of Egypt I called my son" [Hos.11:1]. 16 When Herod saw the magi's trick, he fumed. He ordered killed all male children in and around Bethlehem who were age two or under—gauging from the magi's information. 17 How fully the prophet Jeremiah spoke the Lord's truth when he wrote: 18 "From Ramah comes the sound of loud weeping and wailing—Rachel crying for her children. She can't be comforted. They are no more" [Jer.31:15].* [19] *When Herod died, imagine, an angel of the Lord appeared in a dream to Joseph:* [20] *"Get up; take the child and his mother into Israel. They who hunted him are dead."* [21] *He got up and took the child and his mother into Israel.* [22] *When he heard Archelaus was ruling in Judea in his father's [i.e., Herod's] place, he was afraid to go there. Warned in a dream, he went to Galilee instead.* [23] *He settled in the city of Nazareth. This is another reminder how fully scripture is filled with God's truth, for prophets say, "He'll be called a Nazarene."*

The Covenant offered by God begins, "I, the Lord, am your God. I brought you out of the land of Egypt. You shall have no other gods" (Ex.20:2–3). This describes a God who wants to take care of us. Matthew depicts Joseph as a believer whose trust in God's care led him to relive the original Egypt exile-and-return story [vv.13–15]. He also depicts Herod as one who insisted *he* would take care of things—a pridefulness that caused misery [vv.16–18]. Matthew describes Joseph trusting the Lord's word that it was safe to return [vv.19–21], and trusting the direction to avoid Judea [v.22]. Matthew ends the story with another reminder that the scriptures are filled with stories and sayings that tell us that, though our lives may seem to unfold haphazardly, they nonetheless do so according to a divine plan [v.23].

A note about fulfillment of scripture: in this story, and later in this Gospel, Matthew refers to the words of prophets being "fulfilled." He's not describing the sort of foresight that pundits like to boast about when they look back at their correct predictions. It's a simple way of pointing out that the scriptures now collected as the Old Testament in the Bible speak of God's intention to fulfill the promise of the Covenant—even though the promise often seems to be forgotten [see v.18]. As Matthew unfolds his Gospel, he asks us to notice how Jesus' story reveals that God's promise is being fulfilled.

# THREE

## Baptism

### JOHN PREACHES BAPTISM [MT.3:1–12]

*¹ A time came when John the Baptist was preaching in the Judean wilderness.
² "Repent," he said, "The kingdom of heaven is closing in." ³ The prophet Isaiah
was speaking of John when he said, "A voice calls in the wilderness: 'Prepare
the way of the Lord; make his pathways straight'" [Is.40:3]. ⁴ John wore camel
hair clothing and a leather belt. He ate locusts and wild honey. ⁵ People went out
to him from Jerusalem, from all over Judea, and from up and down the Jordan.
⁶ They were baptized in the Jordan River. They confessed their sins. ⁷ He saw
plenty of Pharisees and Sadducees coming for baptism. "Offspring of vipers!" he
called them. "Who warned you to flee the coming wrath? ⁸ Let your repentance
ripen into results. ⁹ Don't think you can tell yourselves, 'We have Abraham for a
father.' Let me tell you, God can raise up children of Abraham from these stones.
¹⁰ Right now the ax is poised at the trees' roots. A fruitless tree is cut down and
thrown on the fire. ¹¹ I baptize with water for repentance. The one coming after
me is mightier than me. I'm not worthy to help him with his sandals. He'll baptize
you with the Holy Spirit and fire. ¹² He's swinging his winnowing rake. He'll take
the grain from the threshing floor and store it in his barn. The chaff he'll burn in
the undying fire."*

Matthew tells us nothing about Jesus' family life in Nazareth (see 2:23). He leaps ahead here to prepare for Jesus' appearance as an adult. Details of Jesus' past are less important to him than the news that repentance and acceptance of God's kingdom began to be preached by John the Baptist [vv.1–2]. Matthew again notes that certain activities—in this case, John's preaching about reconciling oneself to God's kingdom—have been stressed in scripture. For instance, Isaiah says, "Hear this message, even if it seems to come from nowhere: '*Let* your God get at you! Clear a path for him!'" [v.3].

Matthew says John proclaimed his message with little attention to his need for food or clothing, and that many people heard his message and admitted they were sinners—that is, selfish [vv.4–6]. Matthew describes John addressing warnings about sin to the Pharisees and Sadducees, two Jewish groups dedicated to careful study of the Law. He says John used the image of fruit trees and grain to remind them of the difference between knowing the truth and practicing it. For instance, taking pride in knowing you're a child of Abraham without giving any sign of Abraham's humility and trust is as ridiculous as imagining a fruit tree, without any fruit, bragging, "Look at what a lovely fruit tree I am!" [vv.7–10]. We hear John say, "This plunge into water—this baptism—is serious. It means you truly intend to turn to God. It means you're ready to turn to someone much greater than I am—someone who will plunge you into the fire of the divine spirit" [vv.11–12].

## JESUS ACCEPTS BAPTISM [MT.3:13–17]

*[13] Then comes Jesus from Galilee to John at the Jordan to be baptized. [14] John tried to stop him: "You're coming to me? I need to be baptized by you!" [15] "Let this be so now," Jesus said, "because we should [all] do what's right." John agreed. [16] As soon as Jesus came up from the waters of baptism, imagine, the heavens opened to him. He saw God's Spirit descending to him like a dove. [17] Imagine, a voice from heaven said, "This is my beloved Son, in whom I am well pleased."*

━━◦∕∕∕◦━━

As Matthew reports this event, Jesus' attitude and John's reception of him contrast vividly with the encounter between John and the Pharisees and Sadducees in the previous scene. Matthew doesn't say how John recognized Jesus as the "one mightier" than he (see 3:12). He simply tells us that John thought it would be fitting for him to be ritually plunged into divine life by Jesus, rather than the other way around. Then we hear Jesus say baptizing him was fitting because it was right for everyone to recognize their need to turn to God. The Covenant that God offers is a relationship in which he cares for us (see comments above on 2:13–15). Matthew is making it clear that Jesus wants to accept that divine care [vv.13–15].

Matthew then tells us that, after Jesus used John's baptism of repentance to give witness that he gladly accepted the relationship offered by God in the Covenant, the sky seemed to break open, and God's Spirit rushed upon Jesus like a dove rocketing to its roost; then a celestial voice responded to Jesus' witness with a declaration of love and delight [vv.16–17]. Although this moment could be treated cinematically with elaborate and startling effects, it's presented by Matthew quite straightforwardly: like a child, Jesus turns wholeheartedly to God; and God says, "I love you, my child"; and he fills him with his Spirit.

If we think the signs of God's presence and approval described by Matthew are extraordinary, even unlikely, perhaps we're thinking of God's response to our own expressions of repentance. If the sky never opens, and we never feel the Spirit's rush, or hear God's voice, what does that tell us? Might our repentance, like that attributed to the Pharisees (see 3:7–8), be a mere formality? That would be bad news. However, it would be Good News to be invited to learn from Jesus how to turn to the Father wholeheartedly and with complete trust. If we did that, we'd see and hear the same things Jesus heard and saw.

# FOUR

## Turning to the Father

*¹ [After the baptism,] the Spirit led Jesus to the wilderness to be tempted by the devil. ² He fasted forty day and nights. So, he was hungry. ³ The one who tempts came close and said, "If you're the Son of God, tell these stones to become bread." ⁴ "It's written," he answered, "'One doesn't live on bread alone, but by each word from God's mouth' [see Dt.8:3]." ⁵ The devil then takes him to the holy city and puts him on top of the Temple. ⁶ "If you're the Son of God," he said, "Fling yourself down. For it's written: 'He'll give your care to his angels. They'll take you in their hands to keep you from tripping on a stone' [Ps.91:11–12]." ⁷ "It's written," said Jesus, "'Don't put the Lord, your God, to the test' [Dt.6:16]." ⁸ Next, the devil takes him high on a mountain to point out the splendors of the world's kingdoms. ⁹ He said, "I'll give you all these things, if you bend down and give me homage." ¹⁰ "Go away, Satan," said Jesus. "It's written: 'You will give homage to the Lord. Him alone will you serve' [Dt.6:13]." ¹¹ The devil leaves him. And, imagine, angels came and cared for him.*

—◦◦◦—

Matthew says that, as soon as Jesus celebrated his devotion to God by being baptized, the Spirit led him to act out his devotion. We hear that Jesus savored little but God's presence for forty days.

Then he let his dedication to God be tested [vv.1–2]. For example, he was so hungry that he was tempted to ask for an alteration in the plan of creation: "Make stones bread!" But Matthew says he recalled what he'd learned from scripture: "True nourishment comes not from food, but from God" [vv.3–4]. The Father of Lies can also cite scripture, so Matthew tells us he suggested that Jesus should make God care for him. But we hear that Jesus also learned from scripture that, if you trust God, there's no need to test him [vv.5–7].

Next, we hear the devil make an offer that, logically, shouldn't be tempting: "Adore me, the Father of Lies, and give yourself over to deceit and delusion so that you can have all the world's glories" [vv.8–9]. In essence, he's saying, "Only if you're deluded can you be satisfied." But, if that proposition seems obviously laughable, notice that Jesus isn't described as laughing. We see him calling to mind what's true—in this case, the truth that life consists in serving God, not oneself—not simply rejecting what's fraudulent. Matthew once more depicts him recalling scripture [v.10].

As Matthew has described it here, Jesus' habit of repeatedly savoring God's word in scripture helped him to turn from distractions and to be filled with consolation [v.11]. This could be Good News for anyone else who needs to keep learning how to reject the lure of bad deals.

## JESUS TEACHES OTHERS TO TURN TO THE FATHER—TO REPENT [MT.4:12–25]

*12 Jesus heard that John had been arrested, so he moved farther away in Galilee. 13 He left Nazareth and settled in Capernaum by the sea, in Zebulun-Naphtali. 14 The prophet Isaiah spoke the truth when he said: 15 "Land of Zebulun, Land of Naphtali, you, route to the sea northwest of the Jordan, to Galilee of the Gentiles! 16 Your people abided in darkness. Now they see a great light. In the land shadowed by death rises the light" [see Is.8:23–9:1]. 17 Jesus then started to preach: "Repent. The kingdom of heaven is closing in." 18 As he walked along the Sea of Galilee, he saw two brothers, Simon (called Peter) and Andrew, casting a net into the sea. They were fishermen. 19 "Come," he says; "follow me, and I'll*

make you fishers of men." <sup>20</sup> *They immediately left the net and followed him.*
<sup>21</sup> *Moving on, he saw two other brothers, Zebedee's sons, James and John. They
were in a boat with their father, Zebedee, mending nets. He called them.* <sup>22</sup> *They
immediately left their boat and father, and followed him.* <sup>23</sup> *He went all over
Galilee. He taught in their synagogues, proclaimed the Good News of the kingdom, and healed every disease and illness among the people.* <sup>24</sup> *Rumors about
him spread north, through Syria. They brought him anyone who was ill or in
distress from pain, possession, lunacy, or paralysis. And he healed them.* <sup>25</sup> *Great
crowds followed him, coming from Galilee, the Decapolis, Jerusalem, all Judea,
and Syria (beyond the Jordan).*

Matthew describes a rush of activity leading up to and resulting
from Jesus' first preaching—beginning with the report of John's arrest in Judea, south of Nazareth, which apparently prompted Jesus'
move north to Capernaum by the Sea of Galilee. Though Capernaum was hardly the middle of nowhere, it was far from Jerusalem,
the city of light set on a mountain. But, as Isaiah says, divine light
can shine anywhere, penetrating into even the darkest of places
[vv.12–16]. Matthew says Jesus taught that, to enjoy the warmth of
the divine light, all you need to do is turn and accept it [v.17].

Jesus' first invitations to follow him are reduced to details that
make only one point: some people dropped everything—even family ties—to find out what he had to teach. This overturns what we
think of as normal behavior [vv.18–22]. Without giving us time to
reflect on this extraordinary conduct, Matthew next tells us what
Jesus taught and did: he traveled all over; he said God's kingdom
was very close; he responded to people's distress by relieving it
[v.23]. People came from distant regions, such as Syria, and Jesus
greeted all their suffering with the same response: he healed them
[vv.24–25]. Matthew doesn't say whether people were attracted to
him because of his Good News, or his healing—or both.

# FIVE

## Jesus Teaches on the Mountain

### REASONS TO REJOICE [MT.5:1–12]

*¹ Jesus responded to the crowds by climbing the heights [above the shore of the Sea of Galilee] and sitting there to teach. His disciples gathered close. ² He began to express his teaching this way: ³ "How happy are the needy! Their kingdom is the kingdom of heaven. ⁴ How fortunate are the mournful! They'll be glad. ⁵ So blest are the lowly! They'll inherit the earth. ⁶ How blest are those who hunger and thirst for what's right. They'll be satisfied. ⁷ How happy are the merciful! They'll get mercy! ⁸ So fortunate are the pure hearted! They'll see God. ⁹ How blest are peacemakers—children of God! ¹⁰ Blest are the harassed who do the right thing! The kingdom of heaven is theirs. ¹¹ You're fortunate when you're upbraided and harassed by others—when they revile and slander you because of me. ¹² Rejoice! Be glad! Your yield in heaven will be huge. Before your time, they treated the prophets the same way."*

—❦❦❦—

Matthew's description of Jesus' ascent to the mountain creates the image of someone positioning himself to be heard, indicating that anyone who wanted to listen should gather around. Matthew says those who had decided to follow him, such as Peter, Andrew,

James, and John, did draw near. But others were obviously welcome to attend [vv.1–2].

The eight "beatitudes" with which Matthew describes Jesus beginning his teaching [vv.3–10] condense the message contained in the scriptures of the Old Testament. They summarize the benefits of accepting the Covenant. Each exclamation is a variation on a cry of rejoicing in God's promise to give himself to us: "You will indeed be blessed with God's kingdom, consolation, creation, perfection, graciousness, glory, and peace if you need these blessings." How simple—unless you don't like being needy.

We're tempted to answer our needs with our own wits—just as Jesus was tempted (see 4:3–10). Here, Matthew describes Jesus teaching what he learned during temptation: "Let your needs press in on you; notice how you'd like to take care of them; then remember God's care, and accept it." If we saw ourselves as infinitely needy, we'd seek infinite help—that is, God's help.

As Matthew describes it, Jesus' teaching might seem so absurd to those who prize self-sufficiency that it will provoke them to ridicule anyone who accepts it. But didn't the prophets get that reaction when they told the truth? We hear Jesus tell us to rejoice and be glad to be blessed with the realization of that truth [vv.11–12].

## REJOICING SHOULD BE EXPRESSED AND TAUGHT [MT.5:13–20]

*[13] As Jesus continued to teach, he said, "You're the earth's salt. If salt ever lost its zest, how would it get it back? It would be good for nothing but gravel on a footpath. [14] You are light for the world. You don't build a city on a mountain to hide it. [15] And you don't light a lamp to put under a basket, but on a stand to light the house. [16] So, let your light shine. Let others see the good you do so they can glorify God. [17] Don't think I came to undo the Law or prophets. I come not to undo, but to fulfill. [18] O yes, indeed, I tell you, not before heaven and earth expire will the smallest part of one letter of the Law expire—not before everything is complete. [19] So, anyone who dismisses the smallest of commands, and teaches others to do so, will be treated as the smallest in the kingdom of heaven. But*

*whoever follows them and teaches others about them will be considered great in the kingdom of heaven.* <sup>20</sup> *I tell you, if you can't do things more righteously than the scribes and Pharisees, you'll never enter the kingdom of heaven."*

Matthew just depicted Jesus stressing the importance of finding joy in God's blessings (see 5:11–12). Now we hear Jesus tell his followers not to bottle up or tamp down that joy, but to express it exuberantly [vv.13–15]. If they let the world see how good it is to turn to the Lord, others will say, "God seems to be at work here!" [v.16]. We also hear Jesus tell them not to think that this teaching is wild or new; he's simply talking about fulfilling the terms of the relationship described in the Law and prophets [v.17].

The Law—that is, the Bible's first five books, collectively called the Torah—explains that God created the world and offered us a Covenant to help humans become full sharers in creation. This Covenant is summarized in the commandments that describe what people were to do if they accepted God's offer to be his people (see Ex.6:7; 20:2ff.). The prophets were those who called on the people of God to live out their part of the divine deal—that is, to keep the commandments. Jesus, according to Matthew, not only saw himself in the prophetic tradition of calling people back to accept the Covenant but also saw that the whole purpose of life was to learn to delight in the Covenant. We hear Jesus say that only when this world is over will the time of learning the Covenant be over; until then, we'll need to keep studying the instructions for living in it [v.18].

Matthew also describes Jesus saying he wanted his disciples to share his prophetic voice and message: "Teach others about the Covenant! Cherish and share this deal!" [v.19]. Matthew depicts Jesus warning that some Jewish scholars and teachers of the Law— scribes and Pharisees—didn't teach the Covenant properly. True disciples will get it right [v.20].

## HOW TO REJOICE IN THE COVENANT [MT.5:21–26]

*21 Jesus kept teaching about the Covenant: "You learned what our ancestors learned: 'You shall not kill' [Ex.20:13]; 'Whoever commits murder incurs judgment' [Ex.21:12]. 22 But I tell you, all who are angry with others incur judgment. If you call your brother a fool, you'll answer to the representatives of the whole community. If you call your brother an idiot, you put yourself in eternal fire. 23 Now, say you're bringing an offering to the altar but remember that someone has a grievance with you. 24 Leave the gift. Go be reconciled. Then offer your gift. 25 Work things out with your creditor as you head to court. Once the creditor accuses you before the judge, the judge will hand you over to the bailiff for imprisonment. 26 O yes, indeed, I say you won't get out until you pay the last coin."*

Jesus has just been described telling his disciples and anyone else who was listening that they must know and savor the demands of the Covenant (see 5:19). Now we hear him explaining what it means to actually follow the commands that spell out our part in the Covenant. He reviews what the disciples already know: they have no right to take a life, and God judges those who do [v.21]. But Matthew describes him pushing them to understand what it means to respect the lives of others, asking them to note that hot, murderous feelings are judged just as harshly by God as deadly deeds. Matthew says Jesus used the image of standing accused before the whole community—the Sanhedrin being the council of official representatives of the Jewish community—even for hostile words to a fellow member of the community. Then we hear Jesus add: "You're responsible for the hell you create for yourself when your heart is full of hate" [v.22].

Matthew says Jesus went on to tell them that letting go of a grudge and reconciling with an enemy was necessary before ritual worship could be meaningful. Praising God is empty if you're not reconciled with others [vv.23–24]. Then Matthew describes Jesus using an image familiar to fans of crime stories. When detectives are trying to convince suspects to confess, they warn them that once they ask for a lawyer (in the hope of avoiding any responsibility for some misdeed) they'll be pulled into a relentless legal process—and they won't like being steamrolled by the law. They're encouraged to admit their mistakes and then work out a deal that brings some sort of justice. We hear Jesus make a similar appeal to common sense, presenting his disciples with a choice: accept responsibility for seeking peace with your adversaries, or take the chance that someone will call for the strictest of judgments to be pronounced on you [vv.25–26].

## KEEPING PROMISES, TAKING OATHS [MT.5:27–37]

[27] *Jesus continued teaching about the Covenant. "You've been taught: 'You shall not commit adultery' [Ex.20:14].* [28] *But I tell you, anyone who looks at another with lust is already an adulterer at heart.* [29] *If your right eye leads you to sin, tear it out and throw it away. Better to lose part of you than be hurled whole into the torment of Gehenna—a fire that won't stop burning.* [30] *If your right hand leads you to sin, cut it off and throw it away. Better to lose part of you than to head off in one piece to torment in Gehenna.* [31] *It's said, 'Whoever divorces should provide a document of divorce' [see Dt.24:1–4].* [32] *I say anyone who divorces a wife— unless it was a wrongful union—makes her commit adultery. And anyone who marries a divorced woman commits adultery.* [33] *You've also learned that your ancestors taught: 'You shall not swear falsely' [see Lv.19:12]; and you must fulfill the promises you make before the Lord.* [34] *I say don't swear at all! Not by heaven, God's throne;* [35] *not by the earth, God's footstool; not by Jerusalem, the city of the divine king.* [36] *And don't swear by your head, where you can't even control hair color!* [37] *Let 'Yes' mean yes; 'No' mean no. The impulse to add more is evil."*

Here Matthew says Jesus continued to explain that the commands of the Covenant demand more than a display of observance. He tells us Jesus reminded his hearers that no one should declare life-long love for another and then undo the bond. Fidelity must be a matter of the heart as well as a matter of fact. In other words, looking for love as though we knew just how much of it we needed is not only selfish but also destructive. It will foul any relationship— especially the relationship with God [vv.27–28].

The gruesome images of slicing away parts of ourselves put our choice starkly. Do we want the dismal prospect of perpetually look- ing to satisfy ourselves; or do we want the kingdom of heaven [vv.29–30]? Matthew describes Jesus putting this choice another way: "Do you think that, after you give yourself to another, you can redefine the marriage bond by treating it as if it was an ordinary contract for goods and services?" [vv.31–32].

Matthew says the topic moved from marriage vows in particular to oaths in general: make no promise you don't intend to keep [v.33]; don't think you can affect the truth of what you say by huff- ing and puffing with elaborate or high-sounding avowals. Matthew tells us Jesus stressed the pointlessness of pretending to have more power over events than we actually do by noting how little we can do (without dye) about the color of our hair [vv.34–36]. In sum, we hear him say: "If you can fulfill a contract, say, 'Yes, I can.' If you can't, say, 'No, I can't.'" Boasting of your intentions as though you can shape rather than respond to the future is a deadly lie [v.37].

### LOVING [MT.5:38–48]

*38 Jesus continued to speak about the Covenant. "You learned: 'An eye for an eye, a tooth for a tooth' [Ex.21:24]. 39 I say: don't strike back at the violent. If they hit your right cheek, turn the other. 40 If someone demands your shirt, give your cloak too. 41 If they press you into service [carrying goods] for a mile, go two. 42 Give to the beggar; don't turn down a borrower. 43 You learned: 'You shall love your neighbor' [Lv.19:18], but hate your enemy. 44 I say: Love your enemies, and pray for all who persecute you. 45 Be children of your Father in heaven. He brings the sun up for the bad and the good; he gives rain to the righteous and the unjust. 46 What's the great value of loving those who love you? Don't tax collec- tors do that? 47 What's special about greeting fellow community members? Gentiles do that! 48 You should be as perfectly good as your heavenly Father is."*

Here Matthew describes Jesus' teaching turning from contracts and promises to all dealings with one another. The teaching springs from the simple fact that, if we accept a relationship with God who declares that he loves us all, we must come to terms with his all-encompassing love. But how is it possible to love all? For instance, isn't it often difficult for one person in a marriage to enjoy the company of all the spouse's friends?

Matthew says Jesus reminded the crowd that, while the Covenant required a measured response even to those who cause harm [v.38], they should seek more than the demands of strict justice. We hear him tell them to embrace the demands of mercy: "If someone hits you, turn to look them full in the face, but don't hit them back [v.39]. Sympathize with others' needs not only when they're personal [vv.40, 42], but even if you're pressed into public service!" [v.41].

Jesus is described as presuming that, because Jews were taught to love their neighbors, they might think they could despise those who didn't treat them as friends [v.43]. But we hear him point out what the crowd already knew (i.e., they were in a Covenant with a God who didn't play favorites), then ask them to consider the following fact. Many of those whom they viewed as sinners, such as tax collectors (whose supposed dishonesty was obviously selfish) and non-Jews (who didn't accept the Covenant), treated friends well. Did they think the Covenant called them merely to imitate these sinners—merely to be friendly with friends? If, on the other hand, they were truly God's children, did they think there should be some family resemblance between themselves and God? If they were like their Father, wouldn't their loving be perfect [vv.44–48]?

# SIX

## On the Mountain, Jesus Continues to Teach about the Covenant

### WHAT'S THE RIGHT RELATIONSHIP WITH GOD? [MT.6:1–8]

*¹ Jesus continued to speak about what was right. "Don't try to seem 'right,' 'just,' and 'good' to others. What response from your Father in heaven do you expect for showing off? ² So, if you're giving alms, don't blow your horn in the assembly or on the street as hypocrites do. They want honor from others. O yes, indeed, I say that's all they'll get. ³ When giving alms, don't let the left hand know what the right is doing. ⁴ Let your alms be secret. Your Father, who sees secrets, will respond to you. ⁵ And don't pray like the hypocrites who love to stand up in the assembly or on the street corner praying so others will see. O yes, indeed, I say that's their reward. ⁶ When you pray, go to a private room and close the door. Pray to the Father in secret. He sees what's secret and responds. ⁷ Don't babble your prayers like pagans who think grandiloquence gets attention. ⁸ Don't be like them. Your Father knows what you need before you ask him."*

—∽∾∾—

Above, Jesus was described telling the crowd to be just like God, their Father (see 5:48). Here, he warns against trying to impress others with the attempt to do this [v.1]. With examples about pray-

25

ing and charitable giving, he reminds us how tempting it is to convince others of our goodness—and how pointless. If our desire is to
be like God, the praise of others can't help satisfy that desire. But it
can distract us from it because, if others say we're generous and
devout, it's tempting to believe that maybe we are good. It's com-
forting to think that, though "good" isn't perfection, it's certainly
not sinful. But we hear Jesus say that, in the process of making
ourselves look good, we completely ignore God [vv.2, 5] who, after
all, is the only one who knows what each of us needs [vv.3–4].

Matthew tells us Jesus warned his listeners not to start down the
road to general acclaim, for that route would lead to smugness and
complete forgetfulness about one's need for the care of the Father.
We hear Jesus tell the crowd to turn directly to the Father and,
without fanfare, ask for the care he promised to give [v.6]. That's the
right way to relate to your Father.

Matthew says Jesus concluded these comments about convers-
ing with the Father by saying that, whenever you turn to him, turn
with complete confidence that he'll fulfill his promises. You don't
have to give him long lists of reminders about the Covenant
[vv.7–8]. He offered you the Covenant in the first place and knows
all about it. What Good News Jesus gives us about prayer: in
prayer, God does all the work.

## HOW TO PRAY [MT.6:9–15]

[9] *"Pray like this," Jesus told the crowd on the mountain: "'Our Father in heaven,
let your name be made holy. [10] Let your kingdom come. Let your will be as
effective on earth as it is in heaven. [11] Today, give us today's bread. [12] Forgive us
for not giving you what we owe you—just as we forgive what others owe us.
[13] Don't let us get into temptation—rescue us from the evil one.' [14] If you forgive
what others do against you, your heavenly Father will forgive you. [15] If you don't
forgive others, your Father won't forgive you."*

—⚬⚬⚬—

For those who don't know how to keep their prayer brief (see 6:7), or aren't certain how to pray, Matthew says an example was offered. To start off, remind yourself you're in your Father's presence [v.9a]. Then ask for what you need—and notice you're speaking as if all of us share this need. First, ask God to give the gift of regarding him—his very name—as holy, awesome, and mighty [v.9b]. (This will remind us that, since we can't make him sacred to ourselves, we turn to him to do it for us.) Then ask the Father to give us the divine kingdom—that is, to bring to us what we cannot possibly find for ourselves [v.10a]. Ask him to make his heavenly desires effective right here on earth—in our very hearts [v.10b]. Then, to remind ourselves that God is indeed doing what we ask (is indeed filling us with his presence and struggling to fill us with his desires), we should put everyday needs in our Father's hands. Don't even worry about today's food [v.11].

And don't forget how unworthy we all are of these gifts. Recall how often we try to satisfy ourselves—how often we turn away from God. Then we ask for forgiveness [v.12a]. As we ask, we notice how difficult it is for us to forgive others, so we also ask that our impulse to forgive will grow in proportion to our sense of being forgiven [v.12b]. Next, we're instructed to ask for the same guidance Jesus accepted when he was tempted in the wilderness (see 4:1). Because we can't manage on our own, we ask God to keep us from trying to self-manage—to save us from ourselves; to save us from all evil [v.13]. That's it.

Matthew tells us Jesus added a powerful reminder of why we need to turn to our Father for help and care: there's no other way to learn God's impulse to forgive. If we wish to share the relationship God offers us, we have to accept him as he is: forgiving. We can experience his forgiveness only if we're willing to give it as well as receive it [vv.14–15].

## MORE ADVICE ABOUT KEEPING A RIGHT
## RELATIONSHIP WITH GOD [MT.6:16–24]

*⁶ "Do you want to fast?" asked Jesus on the mountain. "Don't be like the doleful hypocrites whose dishevelment says, 'I'm fasting.' General admiration is their reward. ¹⁷ When fasting, fix your hair and wash your face. ¹⁸ Don't advertise your fast to others. Your Father, who sees all secrets, will notice. ¹⁹ Don't pile up goods on earth, where moth and rust consume, and thieves loot. ²⁰ Gather your treasure in heaven, where there's no thief, rust, or moth. ²¹ Where your treasure is, there's your heart. ²² The body's lamp is the eye. If you're clear-eyed, you'll be properly enlightened. ²³ If you're devious, you'll seek the shadows. How dismal to turn light to darkness! ²⁴ You can't have two masters. You'll hate one and love the other, or admire the first and despise the other. So, you can't devote yourself to God and your own treasures."*

———

Matthew says that, in addition to almsgiving and praying (see 6:2–6), Jesus spoke about fasting as another way of reminding ourselves how our relationship with God works. As with every other action, we're tempted to make the act of fasting about ourselves—"You're fasting? You're so conscientious!" [v.16]. Instead, says Jesus, let fasting help you allow God into your life; let it remind you who knows your need for nourishment better than you [vv.17–18].

Then, says Matthew, Jesus encouraged his hearers to make an obvious choice: don't dream of mounds of this world's goods—things that disappear and fall apart—but of everlasting riches [vv.19–20]. This isn't just good practical advice. It stirs up reflections about our deepest longings and asks us how we want to spend our energy. Do we yearn for possessions, or eternal life [v.21]? We hear Jesus put the same question another way by using an image of roving eyes, asking, "What are you looking for; what lights you up? If it's God's electrifying offer to be our God and to care for us always, then you should trust that you'll indeed be filled with divine light" [v.22]. We also hear Jesus warn that, if we work secretly for our own hidden purposes, our selfishness will not bring us light, but lonely darkness [v.23].

Matthew says Jesus used another image to warn the crowd away from trying to snatch God's creative work out of his hands: if you make yourself the master of all your schemes and goals, you can't possibly devote yourself and all your energy to letting God fulfill the divine promises in you. You must choose between the two [v.24].

## ANXIETY ABOUT OUR RELATIONSHIP WITH GOD [MT.6:25–34]

*[25] "So," says Jesus to the crowd on the mountain, "I tell you not to be anxious about life—how you'll eat, how you'll slake your thirst, or how you'll clothe yourself. Isn't life more than food? Aren't you more than your clothes? [26] Look, the birds in the heavens don't sow, reap, or stockpile, yet your heavenly Father feeds them. Aren't you more precious than they? [27] Can any of you use your anxiety to stretch out your life a bit? [28] Then why worry about clothes? Look at the lilies in the field. They grow without working or spinning. [29] Let me tell you, even Solomon in all his glory couldn't dress so well. [30] If God arrays the grasses so splendidly—though they fill the field today and go into the oven tomorrow—how much more will he do for you! So little faith! [31] Don't whine, 'What'll we eat; what'll we drink; what'll we wear?' [32] That's how pagans fret. Your Father knows what you need. [33] Let your first desire be the kingdom of God—God's perfect, right, and just way of doing things. Everything else is included for you. [34] And don't be anxious about tomorrow. Let tomorrow have its own anxiety. There's enough to bedevil us in the present moment."*

Matthew doesn't present Jesus as a Pollyanna who believes that, once we've put trust in God (see 6:24), all will be rosy. Here he describes Jesus speaking of the sorts of distractions he once faced (see 4:3–9). Just as hunger made him wonder how to find food, we too will worry about nourishment and shelter [v.25]. And just as he recalled the promise of the Covenant, he wants us to do the same:

"When you feel anxious, remember that God is taking care of you."
If we need help remembering, Jesus suggests we look at the birds
and plants and notice how creation meets their needs without their
assistance. Do we really think God cares more for birds and flowers
than for us [vv.26–30a]? The honest answer to that question is: Yes!
(We're talking about worry, after all.) Then Jesus names the anti-
dote to fretting: an increase of faith [v.30b].

We hear Jesus say the only thing that casts out anxiety is trust.
Like nonbelievers, we'll find ourselves agonizing about our circumstances. But when that happens, we should review the choice that
belief first presented to us: do you want God's kingdom, or do you
want to build one for yourself? We should then renew our decision
to accept God's kingdom [vv.31–33]. This spells out in detail the
advice with which Matthew tells us both John the Baptist and Jesus
began their ministries: "Repent, for the kingdom of heaven is at
hand" (see 3:2; 4:17). Turning away from self-absorbed anxiety, and
turning to the kingdom, is what we must do day after day after day
[v.34]. All we need will be put in our laps along with the kingdom
[v.33b]. Good News!

# SEVEN

## On the Mountain, Jesus Continues to Teach about the Covenant

### OUR RELATIONSHIPS WITH OTHERS [MT.7:1–12]

*[1] Jesus then said to the crowd on the mountain, "Don't judge, or you'll be judged. [2] The kind of judgment you make, you'll get. Your evaluations will be used on you. [3] You notice the speck in your brother's eye, but don't see the lumber in yours? [4] How dare you say, "I'll get that speck." You have a plank sticking out of your eye! [5] Hypocrite! Take out the plank. Maybe then you can help remove the speck. [6] You don't give blessed objects to dogs nor do you give pearls to pigs— which would simply trample you. (And the dogs would turn and maul you!) [7] Ask, and it will be given. Seek, and you'll find. Knock, and it'll open up. [8] A petitioner receives; a seeker finds; a door opens to the one who knocks. [9] Who will give their child a stone if the child asks for bread? [10] Would you give a snake to one of your children who asked for a fish? [11] If you, who are selfish, know it's right to give good things to your children, doesn't it seem obvious your Father in heaven will give what's good to those who ask? [12] Whatever you expect from others, you should do for them. That's the Law and the prophets."*

—◦◦◦—

Matthew described Jesus telling disciples to understand and proclaim the Covenant (see 5:12, 20), to allow the Covenant to be fulfilled in them (see 5:21–48), and to turn repeatedly to the Father for help (see 6:1–34). Now we hear that Jesus warned against judging others. With comical imagery, he says we shouldn't believe our evaluation of others' faults, but we can believe that our flaws are greater than we think they are [vv.1–5]. Matthew then says Jesus pointed out that we wouldn't thrust something valuable at a pig or a dog lest they react to such strange behavior with startled aggression. Shouldn't we show the same deference to one another [v.6]?

That question might provoke in us a burst of quibbles that come down to one question: "How can I respect those who are annoying?" Matthew says Jesus spoke here of seeking help in prayer. Have a question? Ask. Something missing? Search. Door locked? Knock [vv.7–8]. So, if you need the gifts of patience and respect, ask for them—and remember you're asking your heavenly Father. Matthew says Jesus pointed out how attentive we are to the appeals of our children, and then suggested we imagine God to be at least as attentive as we are [vv.9–11]. Matthew tells us Jesus summed up his explanation of how our relationship with God should shape our relationship with each other by reminding the crowd of the basic message repeated throughout each part of scripture: you'll treat others well if you believe God loves them as he does you [v.12].

## ACCEPTING THE COVENANT MEANS ACTING ON IT [MT.7:13–23]

*13 On the mountain, Jesus kept teaching how to fulfill the Covenant. "Go through the narrow gate. The big gate and wide road lead to ruin—and many head that way. 14 How narrow is the gate and how grueling the way to life! Few find it. 15 Guard against false prophets. They wear sheep's clothing, but inwardly are hungry wolves. 16 You'll know them by their fruits. Do grapes come from thorns, or figs from thistles? 17 A good tree produces good fruit; a sick tree gives tainted fruit. 18 A good tree won't produce tainted fruit; an infected tree can't bear healthy fruit. 19 Trees that fail to produce good fruit are chopped down for the fire. 20 You know the tree by the fruit. 21 Those who will enter the kingdom of heaven aren't those who say to me 'Lord, Lord.' It's only the one who does the will of my*

*Father.* ²² *On the day of entering the kingdom, many will tell me, 'Lord, Lord! Didn't we prophesy in your name, cast out demons in your name, and perform mighty deeds?'* ²³ *Then I'll tell them, 'I never knew you. Get away from me. You work at wickedness.'"*

——∿∿∿——

Accepting God's offer of the Covenant is uncomplicated. It's as simple as saying, "Yes, I will accept your care as my God." But that's not easy. If we believe we can take care of ourselves, and think everyone else should do the same, we may think that we have a rich array of chances for shaping the life we want. Here, Matthew tells us Jesus says the opposite is true. Want true life? Then there's only one choice for you—and it's a choice you'll find difficult to stick with [vv.13–14]. One source of your difficulty will be the prophets of self-promotion who will insist that so narrow a choice is nonsense. They'll tell you to trust your best instincts—to follow wherever your heart leads you. How will you know they're selling bad merchandise? Look at their fruits, their results, says Jesus. Have these false prophets answered the question about controlling life (see 6:27)? No? Then throw out their advice [vv.15–20].

Matthew says Jesus taught that, if you want to reject all other choices and accept his teaching about the Covenant, your response to his Good News will have to be more than a gush of excitement. It will have to show itself in deeds that express praise and gratitude to the Father for offering the Covenant, not pride in yourself for accepting it [vv.21–22]. According to Matthew, Jesus' reaction to those who want to turn the Covenant on its head—"Lord, see how I have taken care of your kingdom!"—will be frank and final [v.23].

## JESUS CONCLUDES HIS TEACHING ON THE MOUNTAIN [MT.7:24–29]

²⁴ *To conclude his teaching on the mountain, Jesus said, "Whoever listens to these words of mine and acts on them will be like the wise builder who built on rock.* ²⁵ *Rain fell, rivers flooded, the wind blasted his house, but it didn't collapse.*

*Its foundation was rock.* <sup>26</sup> *However, anyone who hears my words and doesn't act on them will be like the fool who built a house on sand.* <sup>27</sup> *Rain fell, rivers flooded, wind blasted his house—and its collapse was total."* <sup>28</sup> *When Jesus ended with these words, the crowds were excited by his teaching.* <sup>29</sup> *He taught with authority, not as their scribes taught.*

—◦◦◦—

Matthew says Jesus used the image of choosing a foundation for a house in order to summarize his teaching about accepting the relationship God offers in the Covenant. If we set our lives on Jesus' teachings about the Covenant, our contentment will be like the comfort of weathering a violent storm inside a sturdy home [vv.24–25]. But, if we cobble together other plans, our experience will be akin to the feeling of having a hurricane demolish a house on top of us [vv.26–27]. According to Matthew, the crowd hadn't heard this kind of teaching from their official teachers, the scribes [vv.28–29]—a fact Jesus alluded to earlier (see 5:20).

The image of establishing one's whole life on Jesus' words stresses the importance of accepting his message: the Covenant must shape every moment of your life. Now it's true that, if those in the crowd were devout Jews, they would have repeated throughout each day the prayer that begins: "Hear, O Israel! The Lord is our God. The Lord alone! You shall love the Lord, your God, with all your heart, all your soul, all your strength" (see Dt.6:4–9). But Jesus' teaching, summarized by the first word of his message, "Repent" (see 4:17), asked his hearers to notice that they were not loving God in that way. They had no reason to feel self-righteous [see 7:4]. But neither should they have felt anxious (see 6:33). He could assure them with the authority of his own experience of repeatedly choosing to trust in God (see 3:15–17; 4:10–11) that love of God demands a complete transformation of the heart (see 5:17–48). Matthew reports that Jesus also told people this transformation would require their full attention for a lifetime—during which they should expect plenty of divine assistance (see 6:25–34). The crowd, says Matthew, was deeply moved by this message. Perhaps they heard it as Good News.

# EIGHT

## Jesus Is Sought as a Healer

### A HEALING AS JESUS DESCENDS
### FROM THE MOUNTAIN [MT.8:1–4]

*¹ When Jesus descended from the heights west of the Sea of Galilee [see 5:1], large crowds followed him. ² Imagine, a leper came up, bowed down to him, and said, "Lord, if you want to, you can make me clean." ³ He extended his hand, touched him, and said, "I do want to. Be made clean." He was immediately made clean. ⁴ "Make sure you tell no one," says Jesus. "Go to the priest. Show yourself. Offer the gift stipulated in the Law of Moses [found in the first part of Leviticus 14]. Your adherence to the Law will be your witness to others that you are clean."*

———⟨∕∞∕⟩———

Readers may have forgotten, while reading Matthew's narrative of Jesus' teaching session on the heights above Capernaum, that those crowds had been attracted to Jesus because of his healing as well as his proclamation of the Good News (see 4:24–25). Matthew tells us here that, as crowds continued to follow Jesus [v.1], more healing was sought [v.2]. We can imagine the leper heard Jesus teach, or heard stories about his healings. Somehow he learned the lesson of asking for what he needed (see 7:7). We hear him leaving it to Jesus to present his need to God: "Lord, if you desire this [from God], it will happen." (This is the way we all pray when we ask someone to pray for us: "You will probably be more candid than I would be in telling God how needy I am; so, would you pray for me?")

Jesus is described as responding to this simple request simply: "Of course I will share your desire; of course you'll receive what you need." And Matthew tells us the leper immediately received what both he and Jesus wanted [v.3]. When Matthew reports that Jesus told the man not to speak about this [v.4a], he adds no explanation. But he tells us what Jesus did ask the man to do in response to his healing: he was to give the witness that the Law called for in such a case [v.4b]—that is, he should follow the rituals spelled out in the Book of Leviticus for a child of the Covenant. Though the rituals might seem mystifying to a modern reader, they clearly emphasize that, when those who have accepted the Covenant seek healing from a skin disease, they must remember to turn to God for the healing. Their appeal to God is worship that can be witnessed by the whole community of believers. Jesus wants the man to give this witness. The man doesn't need to tell anyone anything more than what his witness will proclaim: trust.

## REACHING CAPERNAUM, JESUS IS AGAIN ASKED FOR A HEALING [MT.8:5–13]

*⁵ As Jesus came back to Capernaum after teaching on the heights above the lake, a centurion went up to him and made an appeal. ⁶ "Lord," he said, "my boy lies paralyzed in bed with terrible pain." ⁷ "I'll come and heal him," he says. ⁸ "Lord," said the centurion, "I'm not worthy of your entering under my roof. Say the word, my boy will be healed. ⁹ I understand authority—I have soldiers at my command. I say to one, 'Go,' he goes; to another, 'Come,' he comes; to my slave, 'Do this,' he does it." ¹⁰ Jesus was surprised to hear this. He said to those who followed him, "O yes, indeed, I tell you I haven't found faith like this in anyone in Israel. ¹¹ I also tell you that many will come from east and west to recline at table with Abraham, Isaac, and Jacob in the kingdom of heaven. ¹² But the children of the kingdom will be forced outside into the dark, where there'll be weeping and gnashing of teeth.* [13] *Go," Jesus said to the centurion. "Your belief allows it to be so." That hour the boy was healed.*

Matthew's descriptions of Jesus coming down from the heights [8:1] and entering Capernaum [v.5a] create the impression Jesus is heading home (see the next scene). But his responses to the leper [8:3] and to the centurion indicate he considers their needs greater than his. Here, the centurion's concern for his young child's or servant's illness [v.6] is described as moving Jesus to propose changing his destination [v.7]. But the centurion, whom we presume to be a Gentile, won't hear of a visit to his house. First, we hear him say it's not fitting for Jesus to honor him with a visit [v.8a]; then he says it's not necessary. Matthew depicts him believing not only that Jesus will be moved with pity by the illness, but also that he has the authority to heal [vv.8b–9a]. Matthew doesn't describe the centurion asking how Jesus' authority works, but simply accepting that it has real effects—just as he trusts his own authority has an effect [v.9b].

The comparison Matthew says Jesus made between the centurion's faith and the faith of others sounds severe [v.10]. It suggests that Jesus hadn't seen much faith on the mountain (see 7:28) or during his first travels through Galilee (see 4:23–25)—or even in the first response of Peter, Andrew, James, and John [4:19–22]! That suggestion is strengthened when Matthew tells us Jesus painted a very clear image of who would enjoy and who would miss the heavenly banquet [vv.11–12]—to which only the faithful are called (see Is.25:6; 55:1–2; 65:13). Matthew ends this encounter with one final emphasis on faith: Jesus says the man's faith—like the leper's trust (see comments on 8:4)—is what makes the healing possible [v.13]. This is Good News for anyone who is willing to trust God.

## HEALING SHOULD LEAD TO
## TRUST—BUT DOES IT? [MT.8:14–23]

*[14] Jesus entered Peter's house and found Peter's mother-in-law bedridden with a fever. [15] He touched her hand. The fever left her. She got up and started to take care of him. [16] As evening fell, they brought him many bedeviled people. With a word, he cast their spirits out. And he healed anyone who was ill. [17] This showed how fully the prophet Isaiah spoke the truth when he said: "He embraced our weakness; he undertook our distress" [Is.53:4]. [18] Looking at the crowds surrounding him, he instructed the disciples to cross the lake. [19] A scribe came up and said, "Teacher, I'll go with you wherever you go." [20] Jesus told him, "Foxes have holes, birds in the sky have nests. But the Son of Man has no place to rest his head." [21] One of his disciples said, "Lord, please excuse me. I must go bury my father." [22] Jesus told him, "Follow me. Let the dead bury their dead." [23] He boarded the boat, and the disciples followed him.*

—◈◈◈—

Matthew showed us Jesus healing the leper to teach him trust (see 8:3–4), then using the centurion's request for a healing as a lesson to the crowds to let themselves be moved by pity and trust (see 8:8). Here, Matthew depicts a healing so succinctly readers may miss it. And that may be the point. As he describes it, Peter's mother-in-law doesn't gush about feeling better. Suddenly relieved of her needy condition, she was free to attend to the needs of others—and she did so [vv.14–15]. Then, more people sought comfort in their need. Matthew told us Jesus taught that we're blessed when, realizing our need for comfort, we turn to God for it (see 5:3–10), and that we should proclaim to others the blessing of trusting in God's care (see 5:16). Here Matthew writes that Jesus cured many [v.16]. But that's not all. He also cites the Book of the Prophet Isaiah to make the point that Jesus was not correcting God's creation, but fulfilling it. He wasn't getting around our condition of weakness and need; he was embracing that condition [v.17]. Jesus, says Matthew, trusted that God's presence was in our frailty—which may not sound like Good News.

Matthew's description of Jesus' sudden decision to cross the lake [v.18] seems designed to cause surprise: "Where's he going? Isn't there more healing to do?" He then describes two reactions to the decision. First, a scribe volunteers to head off with Jesus immediately. Jesus tells the scribe that, though he sees himself as the "Son of Man"—that is, someone who fully accepts the state of being human—he doesn't worry about things that most of us consider necessities [vv.19–20]. Second, a disciple explains why he can't leave at once. Jesus challenges him to make a choice between serving his family and following him [vv.21–22]. After these invitations to people to free themselves from assumptions they're making about life, Jesus heads off to continue proclaiming the Good News of the kingdom. Some follow him [v.23].

## NO TRUST ON THE BOAT TRIP; NO TRUST IN GENTILE TERRITORY [MT.8:24–34]

[24] *Imagine, as Jesus and his disciples were crossing the lake [i.e., the Sea of Galilee], a big storm came up, piling waves into the boat. He was asleep.* [25] *They went to wake him: "Lord! Save us. We're all lost!"* [26] *"Why are you afraid?" he asked. "So little faith!" He stood up, called the winds and the lake to order, and there was a great calm.* [27] *They were stunned. "What are we dealing with here," they wondered, "when even the wind and the lake obey him?"* [28] *When he landed in Gadarene territory on the other side of the lake, two bedeviled men came at him from a graveyard. They were so dangerous, no one passed that way.* [29] *"What's between us, Son of God?" they yelled. "Isn't it too soon to torture us?"* [30] *Not too far away was a large herd of grubbing pigs.* [31] *"If you cast us out," pleaded the demons, "send us into the pigs."* [32] *"Out!" he said. Out they went into the pigs, which ran into the lake, and drowned.* [33] *The pig keepers fled to the city and told all about the bedeviled men.* [34] *Imagine, the whole city came out to meet him. When they saw him, they begged him to leave their territory.*

Matthew says the disciples were puzzled by Jesus' repose. He also says Jesus was puzzled by their lack of serenity, then asked for the calm they couldn't imagine [vv.24–26]. The disciples seem almost as unsettled by Jesus' response to their fears as they were flabbergasted by his indifference to the storm [v.27]. From Jesus' first appearance as an adult in this Gospel, Matthew has repeatedly portrayed him as placing all his trust in the Father (see, e.g., 3:16; 4:1–4). His disciples, on the other hand, seem to have learned nothing about this kind of trust.

The Gospel According to Mark also describes a boat trip to Gentile territory somewhere on the eastern shore of the Sea of Galilee. Mark's account emphasizes the transformation in one possessed man who, after he's freed from the spirits of self-obsession, accepts a mission from Jesus to spread the Good News about trusting in God (see Mk.5:1–20). Here, Matthew's account stresses the power of our bedeviling spirits of selfishness to resist Jesus' Good News. Matthew says the evil spirits called Jesus "Son of God" [vv.28–29a]—apparently recognizing in him the same dedication to the divine will the Father saw (see 3:17). But we hear these spirits insisting it's not the right time to fulfill God's will [v.29b]. However, if they must bow to the divine will, they choose to abide with mortal pigs rather than with the living God—a choice that's satisfied [vv.30–32].

Matthew says the people of the territory heard these events reported but didn't hear Good News. When they went out to meet Jesus, they saw nothing they wanted, and they asked him to leave [vv.33–34].

# NINE

## What Is Healing, and Why Do We Need It?

### HEALING THE HUMAN SPIRIT [MT.9:1–8]

*¹ They took ship from the eastern shore and returned to his own city, Capernaum.*
*² Imagine, when people brought to him on a mat a paralyzed young person,*
*Jesus saw their faith. "Child, take comfort," he said. "Your sins are forgiven."*
*³ Some scribes muttered, "This is blasphemy." ⁴ Jesus saw what they thought.*
*He said, "Why do you mull over evil in your hearts? ⁵ What's easier: to say, 'Your*
*sins are forgiven'; or to say, 'Get up and walk'? ⁶ I'll help you understand that the*
*Son of Man has the power on earth to forgive sins." Then he said to the one*
*paralyzed, "Stand up. Take your mat home." ⁷ The young person got up and went*
*home. ⁸ The crowds who saw this were frightened. They gave glory to the God*
*who gave such power to us.*

———

The description of the landing back at Capernaum suggests that the
group had scarcely gotten out of the boat before those in need gathered to seek Jesus' aid—in particular, the friends or family of a
paralyzed young person [v.1]. Matthew says Jesus interpreted the
concern of those who carried the youth to him as a sign of faith in
the God who promises to heal all hurt (see, e.g., Is.6:10; 19:22). And

he says Jesus told the youth that turning to God in repentance meant that all previous rejections of God's love—that is, all sins—were forgiven [v.2]. Although this Good News is proclaimed in scripture (see, e.g., Ps.41:5), Matthew tells us that some scribes who heard it from Jesus considered it blasphemous [v.3].

Matthew says Jesus told them they were deeply mistaken [v.4] and asked them to reimagine what healing was—to consider whether God wants us to be well in our souls, or in our bodies. Can someone who believes in the Covenant—in which we are assured we are God's children (see Dt.32:5)—say to another believer: "Your sins are forgiven" or "Your body is healed" [v.5]? Matthew says Jesus concluded with this message: "Take comfort in seeing the healing of a body, and believe that God also delivers your souls from all disorders" [v.6a]. Then the young person was healed [vv.6b–7].

In this encounter [v.6], Jesus is again described calling himself the "Son of Man" (see 8:20). Here, he's teaching that he, a human being who entrusts himself to God's power of forgiveness, shares God's power to forgive. Yet the crowd's response is fear [v.8]. What glory can we give God if we're afraid of his powers? What sort of healthy relationship can exist between an anxious child and a dreaded parent?

## WHO FOLLOWS JESUS? [MT.9:9–17]

*9 Leaving the shore, Jesus saw a man named Matthew sitting at the tax stand. He says, "Follow me," and he got up and followed him. 10 Then, reclining at table at the house with his disciples, imagine, many tax collectors and sinners reclined at table with them. 11 The Pharisees saw this and asked the disciples, "Why does your teacher eat with tax collectors and sinners?" 12 He heard, and said, "The healthy don't need a doctor, the sick do. 13 Learn this: 'I want mercy, not sacrifice' [see Hos.6:6]. I come to call sinners, not the righteous." 14 Disciples of John the Baptist came up and asked, "Why don't your disciples fast? We and the Pharisees do." 15 "The bridegroom's followers can't mourn while he's with them, can they?" said Jesus. "When the bridegroom is taken away from them, they'll fast then.* ⁱ⁶ *You don't sew new cloth on old cloth. It'll shrink and pull the tear wider.* ⁱ⁷ *You don't put new wine in old wineskins. They'll burst, spilling wine and ruining the skins. You put new wine in fresh skins, then both are preserved."*

Scripture is filled with reminders that God wants to be generous to us and doesn't need gifts from us (see, e.g., the story of Saul—1 Sm.). Here Matthew portrays Jesus making the obvious point that those who need God's generosity, especially in the form of forgiveness for their selfishness, must first hear about it. So, he not only calls a tax collector away from a job that requires him to think constantly about himself [v.9], he also dines with him, and shares with him and many others the Good News that repentance and reconciliation can be enjoyed by anyone seeking forgiveness [v.10]. Matthew says Jesus had to remind some Pharisees—scholars of the Law—that scripture describes God offering love, not loving offerings [vv.11–13a]. "Of course," says Jesus, "if you see yourself as sinless, you'll see no need for this reminder" [v.13b].

A question from the Baptist's disciples lets Jesus describe the purpose of righteous works [v.14]. As Matthew relates the answer, Jesus says that if you listen to his words about repentance, you'll rejoice like someone at a wedding feast. You don't need fasting—or anything else—to remind you to turn your attention to the pleasure of the bridegroom's company if the bridegroom is sitting right there with you [v.15a]. If, however, you become distracted from the joy of Jesus' words, then you might need the help of fasting [v.15b]. By fasting, you'd be following Jesus' example of reminding yourself of God's care for you: "I don't need to worry about bread if God's word is my food" (see 4:4). Matthew then says Jesus used two images to point out the need for renewal. In a word, we must abandon our stale prejudices and listen to the ever-renewing word of God [vv.16–17].

## TWO MORE HEALINGS [MT.9:18–26]

*<sup>18</sup> While Jesus was speaking at table in Matthew's house, a local official came in, showed his respect, and said, "My daughter's died; but come, lay your hand on her, and she'll live." <sup>19</sup> Jesus got up and followed him, the disciples after them. <sup>20</sup> Imagine, a woman who'd hemorrhaged for twelve years went up to touch his cloak. <sup>21</sup> "If I can just touch his cloak," she thought, "I'll be healed." <sup>22</sup> Jesus turned, saw her, and said, "Take comfort. Your faith heals you." Right then, she was healed. <sup>23</sup> Jesus reached the official's house to find flute players and a wailing crowd. <sup>24</sup> "Go away," he said. "The girl hasn't died. She's sleeping." They laughed at him. <sup>25</sup> But he put them out, went in to the girl, took her hand, and raised her. <sup>26</sup> A report of this spread through all the area.*

Matthew suddenly picks up the pace by succinctly narrating two acts of healing in which Jesus' reactions were swift and simple. To our ears, the official (who, unlike the centurion, sees nothing wrong with Jesus coming to his house—see 8:8—and may therefore be a Jewish official) may seem to ask the impossible for his daughter. But Matthew hints at no hesitation in Jesus' response to him [vv.18–19]. Then, with a brief mention of Jesus' departure with the official, we quickly find ourselves in the middle of another scene with a woman whose vaginal bleeding would have made her an outcast. She hopes to end twelve years of torment with a touch of cloth [vv.20–21]. Before we have time to weigh our reactions to her bold hopes, Jesus has recognized her trust and has begun to comfort her with the Good News that faith brings healing. And she was healed [vv.20–22].

With another quick shift, we're at the official's house in the middle of organized mourning [v.23]. According to Matthew, Jesus didn't whisper a polite request for calm but told the paid musicians and grieving crowd they'd made a mistake and could go home [v.24a]. The crowd is described as certain of their understanding of death and, thus, reduced to incredulous laughter [v.24b]. Matthew doesn't show us Jesus inviting the crowd to stay and learn something different about death, but simply getting them to leave [v.25]. Then, says Matthew, Jesus did what the crowd was certain couldn't be done: he raised the girl to life [v.26].

Matthew doesn't say what things were said when the report of this incident spread all around [v.26]. People might have said, "Well, that settles it; now I see how little I know about life. I'll never trust myself again; I'll put all my trust in God." Or, they may have said, "How did he do that?"

## FAITH EXPRESSES ITSELF IN CRIES FOR HELP AND HEALING [MT.9:27–38]

*27 As Jesus left the official's house, two blind men followed him, crying out, "Take pity on us, Son of David." 28 When he got back to Peter's house, they came up to him. "Do you believe I can do this," he asked. "Yes, Lord," they said. 29 He touched their eyes. "Because of your faith, so let it be for you." 30 And their eyes opened. Jesus insisted strenuously, "Don't let others know this." 31 But they went off and talked about him all over the area. 32 As they left, others brought in a bedeviled man who couldn't speak. 33 Once the demon was cast out, the mute man spoke. The crowds were amazed and said, "This never happened before in Israel!" 34 But the Pharisees said, "He casts out demons through the ruler of demons." 35 Jesus left Capernaum and went to cities and towns all around to teach in their synagogues, preaching the Good News of God's kingdom, healing disease and distress. 36 He was moved with pity for the crowds. They were like frightened sheep without a shepherd. 37 He said to the disciples, "There aren't many workers for such a great harvest. 38 Ask the Lord of the harvest to send out harvesters."*

In two short scenes, Matthew describes people responding to miracles with such shock that they seem to miss Jesus' Good News—the news that God's blessings are truly available to all who ask for them. Earlier, Matthew portrayed Jesus teaching that we are being blessed when we feel the need to turn to God in trust (see 5:3–10). In the first scene here, where two blind men hail Jesus as "Son of

David" [v.27], what sort of blessing were they seeking? Matthew doesn't say whether the men thought of David as an extraordinarily powerful king, or as someone whose power came from his trust in God. But when Matthew says Jesus told them to remain silent [v.30b], he seems to suggest that Jesus suspects they won't describe their healing as a reminder that one can place total trust in God. When the men ignored Jesus' command not to speak of their healing, did they go about proclaiming Good News about the blessings of God's kingdom, or did they speak about their healing as an amazing bit of luck?

Matthew has described crowds around Jesus as needy individuals seeking aid (see 4:23–25; 8:1–2, 16–17; 9:2). And he's told us Jesus taught that divine aid was given to all who asked for it. In the second scene here, a group is amazed when their request is answered [vv.32–33]. The group expresses their incredulity by noting how rare miracles are, while some Pharisees say the miracle is a trick [v.34]. Neither group wonders whether God might have been doing what God has always promised to do: care for them.

According to Matthew, Jesus encountered this muddled mix of neediness, bedevilment, distress, and skepticism when he returned to his travels (see 4:23) to proclaim the Good News [v.35]. Deeply moved by people's needs, Jesus encouraged his disciples to join him in asking for divine help in responding to these needs [vv.36–38].

# TEN
## The Task of a Disciple of Jesus

JESUS COMMISSIONS TWELVE DISCIPLES [MT.10:1–4]

*¹ After Jesus spoke about the need to spread the Good News, he called his twelve disciples to him. He gave them power to cast out demons, and to heal all disease and distress. ² The names of these "apostles" [i.e., individuals "sent to speak on another's behalf"] are, first of all, Simon, the one nicknamed Peter; and Andrew, Peter's brother; and James-son-of-Zebedee, and his brother, John; ³ Philip, and Bartholomew; Thomas, and Matthew-the-tax-collector; James-son-of-Alphaeus, and Thaddaeus; ⁴ Simon-the-Cananean; and Judas Iscariot, who betrayed him.*

———✸———

Matthew offers no explanation for Jesus' choice of these twelve men to share his mission of spreading the Good News of renewal and healing. While it's natural for readers to suspect that the number twelve may have some symbolic significance, Matthew mentions none. The author of this Gospel may simply have set the number of disciples at twelve because earlier Gospel accounts had done so (see, e.g., Mk.4:14–19). Whatever Matthew's reason for choosing it, the number certainly helps to make the narrative's point that Jesus wanted to send out a sizable number of people to proclaim the

Good News (see 9:37–38). More important to Matthew than the number of disciples sent is the power with which Jesus sends them: the power to free people from their demons and relieve them of all ills [v.1b].

Although Matthew's list identifies twelve specific disciples [vv.2–4]—distinguishing one Simon from another, for example, and noting the different fathers of two men named John—he offers no brief biographies to flesh out their identities. Although we'll read more about a few of them, we know nothing about most of them. Matthew's point seems to be that real human beings with individual lives as different from one another as a fisherman and a tax collector were called by Jesus to do what he was doing; and they accepted the call. In other words, the author isn't interested in telling stories about the disciples, but about what they were called to do. And, far from emphasizing their willingness or ability to accomplish the mission on which Jesus sends them, he ends his list with a startling example of their failure. He says Jesus asked a man to spread the Good News of repentance who, instead of turning to God, turned to betrayal.

## INSTRUCTIONS FOR DISCIPLES [MT.10:5–15]

[5] *Jesus sent the twelve off with these instructions: "Don't head to the Gentiles or into Samaritan cities.* [6] *Instead, go to the lost sheep of Israel.* [7] *Wherever you go, preach the Good News that, 'The kingdom of heaven is close.'* [8] *Heal the sick. Raise the dead. Cleanse lepers. Cast demons out. You received these as gifts, give them as gifts.* [9] *Don't keep coins in your purse; don't carry a travel bag.* [10] *Don't have a second shirt, or sandals, or a staff. Workers, however, deserve food.* [11] *When you go to a city or town, find out who's worth speaking to. Stay with them until you leave.* [12] *Greet their household with the blessing of peace.* [13] *If the house is worth your witness, let your peace rest on it. If not, keep your peace.* [14] *If they reject or ignore your words, leave the house—or city—and dust off your feet.* [15] *O yes, indeed, I tell you Sodom and Gomorrah will have it easier than that place on the day of judgment."*

—*☙☙☙*—

Matthew told us Jesus wanted his disciples to be as moved by the plight of their fellow Jews as he was (see 9:36b). Here he describes him telling them to look for those who, though invited by the Covenant to abide in God's care, appear to be "lost sheep" [vv.5–6]. When they found such people, their task was simple: they should tell them they were not lost, and that, in fact, God's kingdom was very close to them [v.7]. The apostles should celebrate the renewal proclaimed by the Good News by freely sharing the blessings of healing they had experienced [v.8b].

To cynics, Jesus' commission may sound like a fool's errand. If people had lost sight of the Covenant, how would news of an unseen kingdom help them rediscover it? And realists might wonder: was Jesus' command to heal illnesses, raise the dead, and free people from demons—and, oh yes, to expect to be fed for one's pains—truly all that was needed for this mission [vv.8a, 9–10]? Matthew describes Jesus addressing these worries: "Seek only willing listeners [v.11]; if you find an interested audience, relish the comfort of their enthusiastic reception [vv.12–13a]; if you meet resistance, don't be anxious, but remain peaceful and then move on, not letting yourselves be burdened even by the dust of the place where you found no one ready to repent" [vv.13b–14].

These instructions stress that the purpose of spreading the Good News is simply to invite people to hear it. No special equipment or special pleading is necessary. Here we see Jesus freeing his disciples from any need to judge the results of their efforts. That, after all, can be truly known only by God. They can therefore leave judgment to God [v.15].

## HOW SHOULD DISCIPLES DEAL WITH OPPOSITION? [MT.10:16–23]

[16] *To the disciples he'd commissioned, Jesus said, "Look, I'm sending you like sheep among wolves, so you must be as smart as snakes but as harmless as doves.* [17] *Be careful of others. They'll turn you in to the community councils;*

*they'll thrash you in their synagogues. [18] They'll haul you before governors—before kings!—because of me. This is your witness to them, even to the Gentiles. [19] When they arrest you, don't worry about what to say or how to make your case. You'll have the gift of what to say at the hour you need it. [20] You're not the one speaking! Your Father's Spirit is speaking in you. [21] Brother will give up brother to death; fathers, their children. Children will turn against parents to have them killed. [22] You'll be hated by all because of my name. But if you persevere, you'll be saved. [23] When they persecute you in one place, flee to another. Listen to what I tell you: You won't get around to all the places in Israel before the Son of Man comes."*

Matthew lets us know that Jesus emphasized the dangers his disciples would face on their mission, stressing the need to watch out for trouble, but warning against combativeness [v.16]. We hear him tell them they should be prepared for the Good News to provoke not only resistance but punishment from Gentile authorities as well as Jewish officials [vv.17–18a]. But they should consider their humiliating treatment as a witness to their belief in Jesus' teaching—even to the Gentiles [v.18b]. To hammer home the point that this mission depends on a willingness to testify to the truth, not a knack for making a good impression, Matthew says Jesus told the disciples not to fret about defending themselves or their message. Because the message was not their own but an announcement of the same Good News Jesus was inspired to proclaim in his actions and his words (see 3:13–15; 4:17), they should expect to be moved by the same Spirit that moved Jesus (see 3:16; 4:1) whenever they share his message [vv.19–20].

The rest of Jesus' preparation of the disciples may sound discouraging, for we hear him say their message will provoke betrayal and vindictiveness even between those whose earthly bonds seemed inviolable [v.21]; they'll find hatred in all corners—no exceptions—because they proclaim Jesus' teaching [v.22a]; they'll be freed from all this acrimony only by persevering patiently [v.22b]. Good News? A concluding statement cited by Matthew notes that there was no timetable for the work of the disciples. They could keep traveling, recording neither success nor failure, until Jesus comes again—at a date unspecified. At that time, the disciples will still be busy proclaiming the Good News [v.23].

## GIVING WITNESS IN THE FACE
## OF OPPOSITION [MT.10:24–31]

*<sup></sup>[24] Jesus continued to prepare his disciples for their mission: "A student isn't superior to the teacher, nor a slave to the master. [25] It's enough that a student be like the teacher, the slave like the master. Now, if they call the head of a house 'Beelzebul,' they'll certainly call household members the same. [26] So, don't be afraid of them. There's nothing concealed that won't be revealed. [27] What I tell you in the dark, talk about in the light; what I speak in your ear, proclaim from the housetops. [28] And don't be afraid of those who can kill the body, but can't kill the soul. Instead, fear the one who can let both body and soul come to nothing in the eternally consuming fires of Gehenna. [29] Aren't two sparrows priced at a penny? Yet, not one falls dead without the Father. [30] Even your hair follicles are accounted for. [31] So, don't be afraid. You're worth much more than sparrows."*

After describing some of the difficulties the disciples will face as they present the Good News to a skeptical world, here Matthew says Jesus reminded the disciples of the resistance and ridicule he himself had encountered—even being called the embodiment of evil (see 9:34). Because he didn't fear such a response, neither should they [vv.24–26a]. Their task was the simple and straightforward business of proclaiming, as he did, the Good News of repentance and renewal. There's no hidden or secret message that their hearers will have to puzzle out for themselves. The disciples have shared private conversations with Jesus as well as hearing him teach various crowds. Matthew says Jesus warns them not to treat what they have been hearing and seeing as hints about a mysterious secret. Speak plainly and openly, says Jesus [vv.26b–27].

Next, Matthew says Jesus spoke of the source of the disciples' ability to spread the Good News without fear: their trust in God's care. Earthly forces can—and, one day, will—end our earthly life. But only God can fulfill his plan to bring us, body and soul, to eternal life. Jesus' disciples can proclaim their belief in the divine plan wholeheartedly and without fear. Or, lacking any trust in the plan, they can reject it and the life it promises—a choice Jesus portrays as a complete rejection of God's hopes that will result in Gehenna, an eternal blaze of regret [v.28]. This is clearly a poor choice, says Jesus, especially since God is such an attentive creator and parent. Matthew depicts Jesus making a kind of joke about the obvious nature of the choice the disciples must make between accepting God's care or refusing it. If God is concerned about all life, including their hair, might that not suggest God has a special fondness for them [vv.29–31]?

## CHOOSE TO TRUST—AS JESUS DOES [MT.10:32–42]

[32] *Jesus continued to instruct the disciples he'd commissioned. "If you speak for me to others, I'll speak for you to my Father in heaven.* [33] *If you disown me before others, I'll disown you before my Father in heaven.* [34] *Don't suppose I've come to bring peace on earth—no, not peace, but a sword.* [35] *I've come to make a clear distinction. [As the Book of the Prophet Micah says:] 'Son against father; daughter against mother; daughter-in-law against mother-in-law.* [36] *Your adversary will be in your own household!' [Mi.7:6].* [37] *If you love your father or mother more than me, you're not mine. If you love son or daughter more than me, you're not with me.* [38] *If you don't pick up your cross and follow me, you're not with me.* [39] *If you find your own way in life, you'll lose your way and your life. If you let go of your life for me, you'll find it.* [40] *If they accept you, they accept me. Accepting me is accepting the one who sent me.* [41] *If people receive a prophet as a prophet, they're rewarded with a prophet! If they welcome a righteous one as a righteous one, they've embraced a righteous one!* [42] *If they give a drink of cool water to anyone in this humble crowd of disciples, listen, I'm telling you they'll be rewarded."*

Matthew stresses that the disciples were asked to speak directly for Jesus [v.32a]. If they spoke as instructed, we're told, Jesus would boast about them to the Father [v.32b] but, if they embraced some other message, they would abandon the divine conversation [v.33]. We hear Jesus tell the disciples he wants the children of God [see 10:6] to face a clear but unsettling choice [v.34]. Matthew says Jesus cited the Book of the Prophet Micah to depict the power of selfishness to pull apart the closest human bonds [vv.35–36], then stated the choice: we can pride ourselves on knowing which relationships are important to us, or we can turn away from pride and, like Jesus, turn to God to learn about the relationship he wants to have with us [v.37]. We hear that embracing God's will, not our own, is a burden—but that it's the only burden worth bearing [v.38].

Matthew says the instruction continued with a warning that those who insisted on shaping their lives for themselves would get thoroughly lost. Then we hear the promise that life would be found by letting it go—just as Jesus does [v.39]. The disciples were again reminded that they were truly "apostles"—they'd been "commissioned" with Jesus' full authority. Perhaps because the point might not seem clear, Matthew's description emphasizes that this authority is the very power of God [v.40]. This point, though stunning, is also obvious: if you welcome a prophet, whom have you accepted? A prophet! If you accept the promise of God to be with you, what have you accepted but God [v.41]? How blessed is the person who treats a bearer of this Good News kindly [v.42].

# ELEVEN
## Jesus Again Teaches Repentance

PRAISE FOR JOHN THE BAPTIST'S CALL
TO WAIT AND WATCH [MT.11:1–11]

*¹ After instructing the twelve disciples, Jesus traveled to teach and preach. ² Meanwhile, John was in prison where he heard about the works of "the Christ." He sent disciples. ³ And they asked, "Are you the one who is to come, or should we wait for another?" ⁴ Jesus said, "Report to John what you hear and see. ⁵ The blind receive sight, paralytics walk, lepers are made clean, the deaf hear, the dead are raised, the poor hear the Good News. ⁶ How blest is the one who is not tripped up by my message." ⁷ As the Baptist's disciples left, Jesus asked the crowds about John. "What did you go out to the wilderness to see—grass in the wind? ⁸ What—to see someone in fine clothing? The finely dressed live in houses of kings. ⁹ What—to see a prophet? Yes. And I say, more than a prophet. ¹⁰ It's about him that scripture says: 'Look, I send my messenger ahead of you to prepare the way before you' [see Ex.23:20]. ¹¹ O yes, indeed, I'm telling you, no one born up to now has been more important than John the Baptist. But the least important in the kingdom of heaven is greater than he."*

⚬⚬⚬

Matthew says Jesus himself continued the work he'd just sent his disciples to share [v.1]—work described as urgent (see 9:37–38). He says Jesus' work prompted John the Baptist to ask whether this was the work of "the Christ" [vv.2–3], the work of the one "anointed" to fulfill God's promises (see Is.34–35). We might see this question as John's way of letting his disciples learn from Jesus—asking, perhaps, "Some disagree with our teacher, John, about what 'the Christ' will do; what do you say?" Matthew says Jesus told John's disciples to notice that his actions were like the actions described in the Book of the Prophet Isaiah's depiction of God's work of salvation (see especially Is.35:5–6)—the work of care and love promised in the Covenant [vv.4–5]. What delightful news (for those who don't resist it) [v.6]. According to Matthew, Jesus then asked the crowd about their expectations. For instance, they surely hadn't traveled into the wilderness to watch grass blow in the wind [v.7]. What, then, had they hoped to find when they went to listen to John? We hear Jesus say that, if their search was for a voice that proclaimed God's truth—the voice of a prophet—their expectations had been more than met. They were exceeded [vv.8–9]. The Book of Exodus and other parts of scripture describe God saying: "Watch! I'm hard at work preparing what's been promised. Wait for it." John added his voice to that call [v.10]. But then we hear Jesus point out that proclaiming and expecting God's kingdom pales in importance when compared to the act of accepting it [v.11]. Below, the implicit criticism in this remark is brought out clearly as Jesus continues to speak.

## WAITING AND WATCHING IS OVER; TURN TO THE GOOD NEWS NOW [MT.11:11–19]

*[11] [Jesus was speaking to the crowd about John the Baptist:] "O yes, indeed, I'm telling you, no one born up to now has been more important than John the Baptist. But the least important in the kingdom of heaven is greater than he. [12] From the days of John the Baptist, up to now, the kingdom of heaven is being overpowered—with the powerful seeming to overwhelm it. [13] But, up to John, all the prophets and the Law spoke out the truth. [14] If you're willing to hear it, hear this: He's Elijah. He's the one who comes before the day of the Lord [see*

*Mal.3:23].* [15] *If you have ears, hear.* [16] *To what shall I compare this generation? You're like children sitting around in marketplaces complaining to others:* [17] *'We played the flute for you, but you didn't dance. We sang a sad song but you didn't break down and cry.'* [18] *John arrived abstaining from food and drink, and they say, 'A demon has him.'* [19] *The Son of Man arrives eating and drinking, and they say, 'Look! A glutton! A wine-drinking friend of tax collectors and sinners!' Well, wisdom is proven in works."*

—————

Matthew just described Jesus praising John the Baptist. Here he portrays him criticizing people's reaction to John's message. Jesus tells them that John was important because he announced God's kingdom, but that accepting the kingdom is more important than announcing it [v.11]. He points out, however, that the kingdom is not being accepted. In fact, from the time John began to point out Jesus' arrival, it's been violently resisted by some powerful people [v.12]. We hear Jesus say, "The prophets spoke truly when they assured people that God would fulfill the divine promise—and even send another prophet like Elijah (yes, John the Baptist!)—to move hearts to turn to God [vv.13–14]. To understand this simple truth, all you need is ears" [v.15].

But people aren't listening. According to Matthew, Jesus compared his listeners to cranky children who, when they can't persuade anyone to play their games, blame their failure on playmates [vv.16–17]. This is the sort of closed-mindedness Jesus finds in the crowd's reaction to the Baptist and himself. The comment about John having a demon suggests that some people interpreted John's passion for proclaiming repentance as a maniacal obsession, and therefore felt free to ignore his call to repent [v.18]. The remark about Jesus' drunkenness suggests that some people felt free to ignore his teaching about repentance and forgiveness because he socialized with those who needed to repent and find forgiveness [v.19a]! The final comment is an appeal to patience, and a warning against quick judgments. Jesus says it's not wise to judge actions until one is sure what the outcome of those actions will be [v.19b].

## HOW TO RECEIVE THE GOOD NEWS NOW [MT.11:20–30]

 *²⁰ After challenging his listeners' resistance, Jesus began to scold the cities where he'd done most of his powerful works, but where the inhabitants had refused to repent. ²¹ "How woeful will you be, Chorazin [just north of Caper- naum], and how sorry you, Bethsaida [just east of Chorazin]. If the miracles performed in you had been performed in the pagan territory of Tyre and Sidon, they'd have repented in sackcloth and ashes. ²² So, I say it will be easier for the Tyre and Sidon territory on the day of judgment than for you. ²³ Now you, Capernaum! Recall Isaiah's words about a pagan kingdom's fall: 'Are you raised to heaven? No, you're brought down to the world of nothing' [Is.14:14–15]. ²⁴ So, I say it will be easier for Sodom on judgment day than for you." ²⁵ Jesus had the impulse to pray: "I thank you, Father, Lord of heaven and earth. You hid these things from the wise and clever, and revealed them to babies. ²⁶ Yes, Father; this is what you wanted." ²⁷ Then he said, "All these things the Father gives to me. No one knows the Son as the Father does. And no one knows the Father as well as I—and those I share him with. ²⁸ All who are weary and burdened, come to me. I'll give you rest. ²⁹ Take my yoke as yours. Learn from me, lowly and humble- hearted. Take it easy. ³⁰ My yoke is easy! My burden's light!"*

Matthew's description of Jesus' frustration with people's failure to accept the Good News is presented not as a complaint but as one more appeal to reflect on the need to repent. Jesus is pictured la- menting that if Gentiles to the north had heard and seen what his fellow Jews had witnessed (see 11:5), they'd have turned to God [v.21] (without even knowing the Covenant). When choices are judged by God, who will be happier, Bethsaida and Chorazin, or Tyre and Sidon [v.22]? And what about Capernaum, Jesus' home base? Despite his teaching and healing there, its people seem not to have considered the possibility that they are sinners who need mending and repentance. Compared to Capernaum, Sodom will seem penitent [vv.23–24].

Jesus' prayer, as Matthew relates it, accepted and rejoiced in God's way of revealing the Covenant: the Good News of healing and forgiveness would become obvious, or be "revealed," to those who recognized their need for it. Those who thought they were wise enough to care for themselves, and were determined never to be needy, would think an invitation to notice their poverty [see 5:3] was nonsense. But, we hear Jesus say God's deepest desire was that we accept our need for him [vv.25–26]. We also hear Jesus telling his listeners that the Father had given him the power to share God's own desire, and that he now wanted to share that power with others [v.27]. Matthew here describes Jesus suggesting that we drop our foolish fantasies ("O, if only . . .") and take on the burden he carries—the hardship of turning to God's desires rather than our own [vv.28–30].

# TWELVE

## Despite More Healing, Jesus Meets More Resistance

### WHAT IS SIN—WHAT IS SERVICE? [MT.12:1–14]

[1] *[After the disciples returned from their mission (see 10:5ff.),] Jesus was walking with them through a grain field on the Sabbath. The hungry disciples picked and ate kernels.* [2] *Some Pharisees saw this: "Look; your disciples do what's unlawful on the Sabbath."* [3] *He said, "Haven't you read what David did when he and his followers were hungry?* [4] *Didn't he enter the house of God and eat the offering bread reserved for priests?* [5] *You know the law that allows Temple priests to break the Sabbath without sin.* [6] *Well, I tell you something greater than the Temple is here.* [7] *If you understood, 'I want mercy, not sacrifice,' you wouldn't accuse innocents.* [8] *The Son of Man is Lord of the Sabbath."* [9] *Moving on, he entered a synagogue.* [10] *Imagine, a man with a withered hand was there. Some Pharisees there, looking for a way to make an accusation, asked, "Can one heal on the Sabbath?"* [11] *He said, "Who here, whose sheep falls into a pit on the Sabbath, won't lift it out?* [12] *A human is more important than a sheep, and therefore worthy of a good deed on the Sabbath.* [13] *Open your hand," he said to the man. He opened it fully. It was as fit as the other.* [14] *The Pharisees left to plan a way to destroy him.*

———≈∞∞≈———

Matthew's previous description of an encounter with the Pharisees
emphasized that group's strict observance of the Law (see 9:10–11).
Here, Jesus is depicted again pointing out the danger of interpreting
the Law narrowly [vv.1–8]. Didn't David's need to eat outweigh the
need for strict observance of a ritual [vv.3–4]? Don't priests, who
serve the people's need to worship, break the Sabbath rule in order
to serve [v.5]? When Matthew says Jesus noted the presence of
"something greater" than the temple [v.6], we're reminded that
worship has no value in itself. God has no use for it. But we must
share it regularly to remind ourselves to turn to God. In worship,
our confession of sinfulness and recognition of neediness should
lead us to be patient with one another [v.7]—just as God is patient
and merciful with us (see Hos.6:6). This teaching of the Son of Man,
Jesus, trumps the Pharisees' strict teaching about the Sabbath [v.8].

Continuing to emphasize the foolishness of trying to find fault in
others, Matthew presents another group of nosy Pharisees anxious
to catch Jesus disregarding the Law [vv.9–10]. As he recounts Jesus'
response to their machinations, we're likely to laugh at their inepti-
tude. How narrow minded they seem to be. Surely they see that
concern for one another is more important than concern for the
rules [vv.11–12]. But Matthew reports that Jesus' concern for the
man with the crooked hand didn't touch the hearts of this group of
complaining Pharisees. Instead, they wondered how they might silence him permanently [vv.13–14].

## GOD'S WORK IS HEALING [MT.12:15–29]

[15] *Jesus, knowing the Pharisees wanted to harm him, moved on. [Wherever he
went,] crowds were attracted to him. He healed them all.* [16] *But he told them not
to talk about him.* [17] *From this we can see how fully Isaiah spoke the truth:*
[18] *"Look: my chosen servant, my beloved in whom my soul delights. I'll place my
Spirit upon him, and he'll proclaim justice to all.* [19] *He won't argue or raise his
voice. They won't hear his voice in the streets.* [20] *He won't break a bent stalk or
snuff a guttering wick as he makes justice triumph.* [21] *In his name all will have
hope" [Is.42:1–4].* [22] *They brought to him a bedeviled man, blind and mute. He*

*healed him. The man spoke and saw.* [23] *Everybody was amazed. They wondered, "Can this be the son of David?"* [24] *But when the Pharisees heard about this, they said, "He casts out demons by Beelzebul, the ruler of demons."* [25] *Jesus saw their thoughts. He said, "A divided kingdom, like a split household, falls.* [26] *If Satan casts out Satan, he opposes himself. How could his kingdom stand?* [27] *I banish demons by Beelzebul? Measure your accusations against the ways of your own exorcists.* [28] *But, if I banish demons through God's Spirit, then the kingdom of God is here.* [29] *(Can you burgle a strong man's house without binding him before stealing?)"*

Here Matthew tells us Jesus moved away from some threatening Pharisees (see above, v.14). Then, moving around Galilee, he asked those whom he healed not to speak of him [vv.15–16]. Matthew explains Jesus' request by citing Isaiah's description of God fulfilling his plans (for all people) quietly and gently [vv.17–21], not with noisy, attention-getting fanfare (see 5:5). But Matthew says that, when Jesus freed a bedeviled man's eyes and tongue, people wondered if he might fulfill their dreams of an earthly king who would be as powerful as King David [vv.22–23]. Matthew says some Pharisees whom Jesus had encountered on his travels were quick to discourage people from expressing any political hopes: "He's the son of a Demon, not of David" [v.24]. We hear Jesus point out that his consistent message of freeing people from bedevilment could be the devil's message only if the devil wanted to overthrow himself—an image designed to provoke laughter. Matthew adds more bite to the humor when he says Jesus asked, in effect, "Is that how people in your group cast out demons?" [vv.25–27]. Matthew then depicts Jesus repeating the Good News he's been announcing from the beginning (see 4:17): for those willing to accept it, the kingdom is here. According to Matthew, Jesus said proof that God's kingdom was indeed present and effective now could be seen in his power to enter where the devil had taken up abode, and evict that trespasser [v.28]. He says Jesus also asked the Pharisees listening to him to consider another proof of God's power at work now: Whom did they think had been overcome when demons disappeared after his exorcisms [v.29]?

## ACCEPTING AND REJECTING GOD'S SPIRIT [MT.12:30–37]

*30 Jesus continued addressing the Pharisees who had accused him of working with Satan: "Anyone not with me is against me. You join me, or you drift away. 31 So, listen to this: you can be forgiven for every sin and blasphemy, but not blasphemy against the Spirit. 32 If you speak against the Son of Man, you can be forgiven. But speaking against the Holy Spirit won't be forgiven either in this world or in the world to come. 33 Grow a good tree; get good fruit. Grow a damaged one; get bad fruit. The crop tells all. 34 Snake spawn! If you're evil, how can your words be good? The mouth reveals whatever the heart harbors. 35 A good person brings good things from their good supply. An evil one brings evil. 36 Listen: every brash word must be accounted for on judgment day. 37 By your words you'll be judged righteous, or be condemned."*

—————

Matthew describes Jesus presenting a choice with life-giving or life-threatening consequences. The Pharisees and others can turn to God for healing and divine nourishment as he does (see especially 4:2–10), or they can lose themselves in a fruitless search for some other source of satisfaction [v.30]. Matthew has portrayed Jesus as someone who allowed himself to be guided by God's own Spirit (see 3:16; 10:20; 12:18, 28). To blaspheme against God's Spirit means to deny the possibility that God can share himself. If you reject God's offer of an intimate covenant, and if you continue to choose not to be related to God, you can't be forgiven for your choice because you aren't asking for forgiveness. You're not seeking to reenter a relationship you've chosen to despise. If you disagree with Jesus as the Pharisees do here, or if you're as slow to believe him as were the disciples (see 8:25–26), you can repent and be forgiven. But if you take no interest at all in believing, you've reached a dead end [vv.31–32].

Then we see Jesus accusing the Pharisees of deliberately encouraging this deadly choice of disbelief. As Matthew describes him, he seems deeply distressed and shocked that these men, who dedicated themselves to studying the Law and explaining the Covenant, would oppose his teaching of repentance, forgiveness, and healing—teachings that are part of the Covenant! By opposing them, they oppose the work of the divine Spirit. Matthew says Jesus used five succinct images to describe their teaching as useless—even dangerous. They're like damaged trees, poisonous snakes, false-hearted talkers, purveyors of damaged goods, and peddlers of twisted truths [vv.33–37]. Their message certainly can't be construed as Good News.

## THE SIGNS OF BELIEVING ARE REPENTANCE AND RECONCILIATION [MT.12:38–50]

[38] *Next, some scribes and Pharisees in the crowd said, "Teacher, we need a sign."* [39] *Jesus said, "You seek signs as an evil, unfaithful generation. You'll get only the sign of Jonah.* [40] *As Jonah was three days and nights in the monster's belly, the Son of Man will be three days and nights in the ground.* [41] *At the judgment, all Nineveh will stand in reproach of this generation. They repented in response to Jonah's teaching. A greater one than Jonah is here.* [42] *At judgment, the queen of the south will rise in reproach of this generation. She traveled far to listen to Solomon's wisdom. Imagine, greater than Solomon is here!* [43] *When a sick spirit leaves you, it looks in the wasteland for rest, and finds none.* [44] *It says, 'I'll go back where I was.' But, coming back, it finds nothing but tidiness.* [45] *It seeks seven worse spirits. They come, settle in, and create a worse situation than before. That's this evil generation."* [46] *As he taught, his mother and brothers stood to the side hoping to speak with him.* [47] *Someone said, "Look, your mother and brothers are waiting to speak with you."* [48] *"Who is my mother," he answered; "who's my brother?"* [49] *He pointed to his disciples: "Behold my mother and brothers.* [50] *Whoever does the will of my Father in heaven is my mother, brother, and sister."*

Matthew depicts Jesus reproaching scribes (official interpreters of scripture) and Pharisees (pious students of the Law) for demanding a sign to affirm what should have been obvious: his teaching about repentance and healing was firmly based on scripture and the Law. They would have known how the Book of Jonah described God's desire to call Nineveh to repentance—a desire so powerful that Jonah, his messenger, fulfilled his mission even after apparently being swallowed up in death. And they'd have known the story of the Queen of Sheba giving up her doubts about God's gift of wisdom after listening to Solomon (see 1 Kgs.10:1–10). Matthew says Jesus warned these teachers that, if they refused to turn away from their assumptions and prejudices, if they didn't follow the example of Nineveh and the queen of the south, they'd be stuck forever with the selfish limits they'd set for themselves [vv.40–42].

Matthew tells us Jesus attributed their lack of openness to smugness, noting that those who prided themselves on being free from sinful delusions, who felt no need to keep hearing the call to repentance, paradoxically opened themselves to more and worse delusions [vv.43–45]. One potent delusion is to presume we know how to judge relationships. The Covenant says all relationships depend on accepting our relationship with God. Here, as Matthew describes Jesus' teaching being interrupted by someone appealing to him to attend to his relatives, we hear once more (see 10:37) a challenge to rethink one of our most cherished assumptions: our notion about family bonds [vv.46–50].

# THIRTEEN

## Back in Capernaum, Jesus Keeps Talking about Accepting God's Word

### A PARABLE ABOUT A RICHLY
### REWARDING IDEA [MT.13:1–15]

*¹ Once, back in Capernaum, Jesus left the house and sat by the sea. ² So many people came up that he boarded a boat to sit as the crowd stood on shore. ³ He told many parables. He said, "Imagine a sower sowing seeds. ⁴ Some sown seed fell on the path and birds ate it. ⁵ Some fell on rocky, thin soil. It sprouted quickly because it had no depth. ⁶ The sun rose high and scorched it, and it withered without roots. ⁷ Some others fell among thorns that choked it as it grew. ⁸ Still others fell on good soil, grew, and yielded grain—here a hundred, there sixty, there thirty. ⁹ Do you have ears? Listen." ¹⁰ The disciples came up to ask why he taught in parables. ¹¹ "All the mysteries of the kingdom of heaven have been given to you, but not to them. ¹² If you already have, you'll get much more. If you don't have, you'll lose even that. ¹³ I speak in parables because seeing, they don't see; hearing, they don't hear or grasp. ¹⁴ In them, Isaiah's saying comes true: 'You hear, but don't take it in; see, but don't notice. ¹⁵ Their hearts are cold; their ears and eyes closed. Otherwise, they'd see, hear, be moved at heart, and turn to me—and I'd heal them' [Is.6:9–10]."*

—⟨⟩⟨⟩⟨⟩—

Matthew has said Jesus spoke of Capernaum's hardness of heart
(see 11:23), and was threatened by Pharisees there (see 12:14–15).
Here he describes him back in Capernaum teaching without fear,
and telling the citizenry a story about the ability of a single seed to
produce, in the right circumstances, unpredictably rich results
[vv.1–8]. Then we hear a note of uncertainty: are the hearers
touched by the story of surprising abundance [v.9]?

The disciples' question that Matthew relates to us suggests they
weren't sure of Jesus' point [v.10]. Because Matthew reported a previous moment of their bewilderment (see 8:25–26), it's possible to
hear Jesus' response to them as a bit of irony: "Surely *you* understand all mysteries" [v.11]. Then Matthew says Jesus pointed out
the connection between hardness of hearing and hardness of heart.
All his listeners, including the disciples, had received countless reminders from his teaching and the teachings of scripture about
God's abundant love and mercy. If they'd truly embraced those
teachings, they'd have sought and found more and more examples
of them; but if they've never truly taken in these teachings, what
little they've learned will dry up [v.12]. Matthew says Jesus told his
disciples they should hear again the warning Isaiah delivered—the
warning Jesus gave when he taught on the mountain (see 7:26)—
"Hear God's promise of healing, and *respond* to it with your whole
being" [vv.13–15].

## JESUS EXPLAINS ONE PARABLE
## AND TELLS ANOTHER [MT.13:16–30]

[16] *[With the crowd still there,] Jesus told his disciples, "You're fortunate if your
eyes see and your ears hear.* [17] *O, yes, indeed, I tell you many prophets and
righteous people wanted to see what you see, but didn't; wanted to hear what
you hear, but didn't.* [18] *Now listen to the parable of the sower.* [19] *If someone gets
word of the kingdom but doesn't take it in, the evil one keeps it from the heart.
That's the seed on the path.* [20] *The seed on rocky soil is one who suddenly
delights in the word,* [21] *but, with no strong attachment, drops it as soon as the*

*word brings insults or suffering. [22] Seed sown in thorns is like listening to the word but letting worldly concern and money worries distract you. [23] Sown-on-good-soil is hearing the word, taking it in, and bearing fruit with hundreds of grains, or sixty, or thirty." [24] He offered another parable. "The kingdom of heaven is like a man who sowed good seed in his field. [25] While everybody slept, enemies sowed weeds in the field, then left. [26] When the grain stalks sprouted and grew, so did the weeds. [27] The man's servants said, 'Master, didn't you sow good seed? Where'd the weeds come from?' [28] 'An enemy did this,' he said. They said, 'Shall we pull the weeds out?' [29] 'No,' he said. 'You might uproot the grain with the weeds. [30] Let them grow together until harvest. I'll tell the harvesters to bundle the weeds for burning but gather the grain into my barn.'"*

Earlier, Matthew described Jesus saying that those who crave God's goodness are blessed to have that longing (see 5:6). Here, he says Jesus answered his disciples' question about telling stories—parables (see 13:10)—by saying that his stories are a perfect expression of his trust that God does indeed satisfy our deepest longing; and his disciples are, in turn, blessed if they share that longing with him [vv.16–17]. Matthew says Jesus then offered the disciples another chance to savor his story [v.18]. He invites them to compare sown seed with God's word and to consider the possibility that, when nothing interferes with the divine word, it is immensely productive [vv.19–23].

Despite the breathtaking nature of Jesus' claims—that his teaching and his example of trust in God were what the prophets and their followers had longed to hear, and that taking in God's word was more fulfilling than any other activity—Matthew moves on without comment to describe Jesus telling another story, about a landowner who was confident that the seed he'd planted would survive, despite weeds that had been maliciously introduced, and who thought the weeds themselves would make a fine fire [vv.24–30].

Below, Matthew will tell us that the disciples required an explanation of this parable too (see 13:36). But here he says nothing about the reaction in the audience. He simply goes on to report that Jesus told still more stories.

## JESUS TEACHES THAT THE KINGDOM WILL COME SLOWLY, BUT SURELY [MT.13:31–43]

*[31] Jesus gave them all another parable: "The kingdom of heaven is like a mustard seed. [32] It's smaller than other seeds, but it grows bigger than other plants, becoming such a large bush that birds can nest in it." [33] He offered another parable: "The kingdom of heaven is like leaven a woman puts in three measures of flour—and it was all leavened!" [34] Jesus said all this to the crowd in parables. He didn't speak without parables. [35] This showed how fully a prophet spoke the truth: "I'll open my mouth in parables. I'll shout things hidden from the beginning" [Ps.78:2]. [36] He left the crowds and went into the house. His disciples came up and said, "Explain the parable of the weeds in the field to us." [37] "The one sowing good seed is the Son of Man," he said. [38] "The field: the world; good seed: the kingdom's children; weeds: children of evil. [39] The enemy who sowed weeds: the devil; the harvest is the end of the age; the reapers are the angels. [40] Just as weeds are gathered for burning, so it will be at the end of the age. [41] The Son of Man will send angels to take from his kingdom tempters and sinners. [42] They'll throw them in the flaming furnace where they'll weep and gnash their teeth. [43] The righteous will shine like the sun in their father's kingdom. Do you have ears? Hear!"*

Matthew says Jesus followed the parable about the weeds (just above) with two other illustrative stories: the kingdom may be as easily overlooked or underestimated as a minuscule seed until it comes to full, astounding flower [vv.31–32]; and, like a pinch of yeast, the kingdom will eventually transform what seems to hide it [v.33]. Matthew says Jesus taught about the paradoxical working of God's kingdom by telling many graphic stories [v.34]—stories meant to reveal what may have seemed mysterious up to then [v.35].

Despite the fact that Jesus' stories seem plain enough for a child to understand, and though his withdrawing from the crowd might suggest he was tired, Matthew tells us the disciples again pestered him for an interpretation [v.36]. Like a patient teacher, Jesus gave one.

It's tempting to imagine Matthew winking at his readers as the interpretation unfolds—as if he's saying, "You're picking this up faster than the disciples, aren't you?" But Jesus' stories aren't riddles that, once solved, are meant to provoke a satisfying "Aha—got it!" Quite the opposite; they're meant to surprise us with what we might prefer to ignore. Here, Matthew makes sure we overhear Jesus telling his disciples that evil will keep flourishing as vigorously as good until the Son of Man, like a smart farmer, realizes the growing process is over [vv.37–41]. Our only task, if we want to enter the kingdom, is to hear Jesus' teaching: Repent; turn to God's kingdom! If we turn elsewhere, our regret will be expressed with unending tears and grimaces [v.42]. If we take Jesus' words to heart, we will be transformed into the likeness of God [v.43].

## JESUS ADVISES CHOOSING THE
## KINGDOM NOW [MT.13:44–58]

⁴⁴ *Jesus told his disciples another parable: "The kingdom of heaven is like a treasure buried in a field that someone discovers, reburies, and then happily sells all to buy that field.* ⁴⁵ *Again, the kingdom of heaven's like a merchant hunting for fine pearls.* ⁴⁶ *He finds one spectacular pearl and sells everything to buy it.* ⁴⁷ *Again, the kingdom's like a net cast in the lake taking up all sorts of fish.* ⁴⁸ *When it's filled and hauled in, they put good fish in crates and throw out the bad.* ⁴⁹ *Just so, at the end of the age, angels will separate the evil from the righteous.* ⁵⁰ *They'll throw them in the flaming furnace where they'll weep and grind their teeth.* ⁵¹ *Do you understand all this?" "Yes," they said.* ⁵² *"So, every scribe who is a disciple of the kingdom of heaven is like a householder who can offer both old and new."* ⁵³ *When he finished these parables, he left.* ⁵⁴ *He went to his hometown. His teaching in their synagogue so amazed them they said, "Where'd this*

*one get such wisdom and miraculous power? ⁵⁵ Isn't this the carpenter's son? Isn't his mother called Mary; his brothers named James, Joseph, Simon, and Judas? ⁵⁶ And aren't his sisters with us? Where did he get all this?" ⁵⁷ They were put off. But he said, "Nowhere is a prophet disparaged but at home." ⁵⁸ He didn't do much powerful work there because they didn't believe.*

We can picture Matthew's presentation of these parables as a review session for both the disciples and us. Do we grasp Jesus' point that the kingdom he's been proclaiming from the beginning is indeed at hand (see 4:17), and that now is the time to turn away from all other choices—to "sell all"—and to accept the kingdom [vv.44–46]? And do we understand that the choice we make will have everlasting consequences, even though it's easy in this present age to ignore the difference between what's right for us and what's wrong for us [vv.47–50]? Matthew tells us that, if our answer is yes [v.51], we'll feel as confident as well-stocked homeowners who know they can satisfy their guests with everything from old-fashioned comfort foods to the latest pièce de résistance [v.52]—that is, they'll be very flexible and competent teachers (scribes).

Matthew then changes the scene, altering the mood from reflective to confrontational [vv.53–54]. He tells us that Jesus' old neighbors in the town where he grew up thought they knew all about him. They knew his father's trade, his mother's name (plus personal history and reputation?), and the identity of all his relatives. They were sure there was some deception or trick behind his confident words and his reputation for powerful deeds [vv.55–56]. The only way they found to make him feel at home, as Matthew describes it, was to boast how they knew him in the old days. Apparently they felt they had nothing new to learn from or about him. Matthew says their denial of his message prevented it from bringing them any good [vv.57–58].

# FOURTEEN

## After a Flashback, Matthew Describes More Traveling and Powerful Work

AN EXAMPLE OF LACK OF FAITH;
JESUS' BELIEF [MT.14:1–21]

*¹ Around the time of Jesus' visit home [see 13:54], Herod the tetrarch heard about him. ² "This is John the Baptist," he said. "Raised from death, he can now do wonders." ³ Herod had imprisoned John because of Herodias, wife of his brother, Philip. ⁴ For John had said, "It's not lawful for you to have your brother's wife." ⁵ He wanted to kill John, but he feared the crowd's reverence of him as a prophet. ⁶ Then, at Herod's birthday feast, Herodias' daughter pleased everyone with a dance. ⁷ In his delight, Herod swore on his honor to give her anything she asked for. ⁸ Prodded by her mother, she said, "Give me John the Baptist's head on a plate." ⁹ He was chagrined, but, because of promising in front of guests, he gave the order. ¹⁰ He had John beheaded in prison. ¹¹ The head was borne in on a plate and given to the girl, who gave it to her mother. ¹² John's body was buried by his disciples, who gave the news to Jesus. ¹³ When Jesus heard, he headed by boat to a quiet place to be alone. But crowds found out and pursued him on foot from several towns. ¹⁴ Landing, he was moved with pity by sight of this throng and he healed their sick. ¹⁵ Evening came, and so did the disciples. They said, "This is the middle of nowhere, and the hour's late. Let the crowds go to nearby villages to buy food."* <sup>16</sup> *He said, "They don't have to leave; you feed them."* <sup>17</sup> *"But all we've got," they said, "are five loaves and two fish."* <sup>18</sup> *"Bring those to me," he said.* <sup>19</sup> *He told the crowds to settle on the grass. He took the loaves and fish. He looked to heaven. He blessed them, broke them, and gave them to the disciples for the crowds.* <sup>20</sup> *They ate, were satisfied, and gathered up twelve baskets of leftovers.* <sup>21</sup> *About five thousand ate—not counting women and children.*

———◦◦◦———

With a mention of Herod, Matthew lets us know that, in addition to Jesus' old neighbors (see 13:57) and the scribes and Pharisees (see 12:39), the civil authority was also keeping a wary eye on him [vv.1–2]. Then, in a flashback about Herod's jittery determination to curry favor with the masses and save face with friends, Matthew shows how our petty but potent anxieties can lead to dreadful decisions [vv.3–12]. Matthew says Jesus went off by himself "when he heard" [v.13a], leaving the reader to wonder whether this refers to news of Herod hearing about him, or to news of the Baptist's murder. The point is that Jesus reacted to some news about Herod by seeking solitude. (We'll read below what Jesus wanted to do in his solitude—see 14:23.)

   Although Jesus' search for solitude is thwarted by others' pressing needs [v.13b], Matthew says Jesus was moved by those needs, not put off by them [v.14] (unlike the disciples who, arriving on the scene, see the needs as a nuisance [v.15] and are baffled by Jesus' suggestions for responding to them [vv.16–17]). Jesus then turns to God with complete faith in his divine care (see Ps.8:5; 144:3); he acknowledges that bread and fish are God's blessings; and he then shares those blessings [v.19]. According to Matthew, because of Jesus' act of faith in the Father, the needs of thousands were satisfied [vv.20–21].

## DO PEOPLE TRUST IN GOD'S POWER? [MT.14:22–36]

*22 After feeding the five thousand, Jesus told the disciples to cross the lake while he saw the crowd off. 23 When the crowd left, he climbed the mountain alone to pray. That evening, he was alone. 24 By then, the disciples' boat was far offshore, buffeted by foul winds. 25 In the bleak hours of morning, Jesus walked to them over the waters. 26 Seeing him walk on the lake, the disciples were horrified: "A ghost!" they shrieked. 27 Quickly, Jesus said, "Take heart. It's me. Don't be afraid." 28 Peter said, "Lord, if it's you, let me come to you on the waves." 29 "Come." Peter leaped over and started towards Jesus. 30 Facing the wind, he panicked and started to sink. "Save me, Lord," he yelled. 31 Jesus shot out his hand to grab him. "So little faith," he said. "Why do you doubt?" 32 When they got in the boat, the wind died. 33 Everyone on board showed reverence. "Truly, you're God's son," they said. 34 They landed at Gennesaret, just south of Capernaum. 35 Everyone recognized him there, and word went around to bring all the sick to him. 36 They asked just to touch the edge of his garments. All who touched were healed.*

Here [vv.22–23], Jesus is described finding the solitude with God that he'd sought earlier (see 14:13). Meanwhile, his disciples were fighting nasty weather. It's not hard to imagine their confusion at seeing someone walk toward them on water they found impossible to navigate [vv.24–26]. As told by Matthew, Peter's response to Jesus' invitation not to fear may seem like a worried challenge: "Give me your powers—then I won't be afraid." Challenge or appeal, Matthew tells us Jesus accepted it, provoking Peter to act [vv.27–29]. But Matthew says Peter became afraid and didn't trust what he was actually experiencing: a sharing in Jesus' power. Although Matthew tells us Peter made an impulsive cry for help, he says Jesus asked him to notice how little faith he had. He apparently saw no reason for Peter to doubt that he could share his divine power [vv.30–31].

As the lake calms, Matthew tells us the disciples reverently proclaimed Jesus' divine sonship [vv.32–33]. But are we to suppose they believed they too were divine children? Is Matthew telling us they learned something about the truth of their relationship with God since the last time Jesus had brought them calm in a storm and noted their lack of faith (see 8:23–27)? From Jesus' first proclamation (see 4:17) through his long first teaching session (see, e.g., 5:48), and in further lessons to his disciples (see 10:40), we've heard a repetition of the astonishing Good News that God's kingdom is here, and that we're meant to share it as God's children. Do we, like the disciples, still doubt this?

The narration moves on to a scene that's become familiar: crowds hear of Jesus' presence and seek healing [vv.34–36]. Were they looking for magic, or were they rejoicing in divine life?

# FIFTEEN

## How Do We See Our Needs—How Does God See Our Needs?

DO YOU NEED TO SEE YOURSELF
AS RIGHTEOUS? [MT.15:1–9]

*¹ Some Pharisees and scribes from Jerusalem tracked Jesus down. ² "Why do your disciples break with the traditions of the elders?" they asked. "They don't wash their hands before they take their bread!" ³ He asked, "Why do you break the commandments of God in order to keep your traditions? ⁴ God said, 'Honor your father and mother' [Ex.20:12], and 'Let the one who speaks ill of father or mother die' [Ex.21:17]. ⁵ But you give this excuse: 'Because my funds are vowed to God, they can't be spent on you; ⁶ so, I do you no dishonor.' To keep your traditions, you make God's word nothing! ⁷ Hypocrites! Isaiah spoke truly of you when he wrote: ⁸ 'This people honors me with lips, but their hearts are far away from me. ⁹ Their worship is pointless—making human rules into commandments' [Is.29:13]."*

———⟢⟢⟢———

Ah, the pleasure of being right! And how easy it is to have that pleasure if you know all the rules. If we find ourselves agreeing with the scholars (the scribes and Pharisees) who noticed the disciples' careless eating habits [vv.1–2], Matthew has lulled us into the sense of righteousness that earlier he described Jesus condemning (see 9:13). When we allow others' faults to seem glaring to us, we can see nothing else—certainly not our own faults (see 7:3). Here, Jesus is described pointing out a trick that clever scholars of the Mosaic Law devised for appearing to treat others according to the commands of the Covenant, while actually behaving selfishly [vv.3–6]. Dressing up sin as virtue is a shameless hoax, mere pious playacting [v.7a].

But this is an old problem. Isaiah, for one, spoke of it. Those who choose to accept the relationship offered by God in the Covenant know what that relationship requires: if they accept God's promise of love and care, they must seek fulfillment nowhere else; and, as they struggle to remain true to this relationship, they must be patient and gracious with all God's other children (see Ex.20:1–7; Dt.5:6–21). And yet, as Isaiah notes, God's children often pretend to respect God's desires while they spend all their energy concocting schemes to satisfy their own desires [vv.7b–9]. Like Adam and Eve, they're tempted to think they have no need of God (see Gn.3:4).

When God's invitation is put starkly—choose life or death (see Dt.30:15)—the response seems obvious. But, if the right choice is so clear, what keeps us from making it?

## EVIL COMES FROM THE HEART [MT.15:10–20]

[10] After addressing the Pharisees' complaint about purity laws, Jesus called the crowd closer. "Listen," he said, "and understand. [11] The things you eat don't contaminate you. The things you say do." [12] His disciples told him, "The Pharisees were offended by what you said." [13] He said, "What my heavenly Father hasn't planted, he'll uproot. [14] Ignore them. They're the sightless leading the blind—blind leading blind to a pit." [15] Peter said, "Tell us what this parable means." [16] "You still don't understand?" he said. [17] "You know what goes in the mouth goes into the gullet, then to the dung pile. [18] What comes out of the mouth—what comes from the heart—is what's foul. [19] The heart causes evil thoughts, murder, adultery, fornication, theft, lies, and blasphemy. [20] Those things make you foul, not eating before rinsing your hands!"

—◦✧◦—

After Jesus called the Jewish officials hypocrites (see 15:7), Matthew says he asked people to recall what ritual ablutions were actually intended to teach: keeping hearts pure [vv.10–11]. After we hear that the officials left in a huff [v.12], we're told Jesus repeated earlier advice (see, e.g., 10:26), and instructed his disciples not to fret about anyone, including a teacher, who doesn't listen or continue to learn. Divine judgment will weed out bad teachers (see 13:40) who are blind to their need for God's mercy and forgiveness [vv.13–14].

Lest we miss this point about our need for divine mercy and forgiveness, Matthew says Peter asked for clarification [v.15], and Jesus again instructed the disciples. The first part of the instruction is easy to understand [v.16]. Although nutritionists might point out weaknesses in Jesus' simple analogy, it's nonetheless clear: food-stuffs are prepared, digested, and evacuated. They don't make us who we are [v.17]. To know who we are, we must examine our hearts. This part of the instruction is also easy to understand, but it's hard to accept. Matthew reports that Jesus said our hearts were the source of wickedness [vv.18–19]. The list of evils seems designed to shock and, perhaps, to provoke a protest: "Surely not my heart!" (see 26:22). But the truth asserted by the list isn't softened by comment or explanation. In fact, it's restated with a nearly comic warning: if you think eating with dirty hands is offensive to others, imagine what they'd say if they could see into your squalid heart [v.20].

This would be unsettling news if Jesus weren't delivering it as part of the Good News—the news that you can repent the selfishness in your heart, and turn to God for healing (see Ps.51:12).

## FAITH COMES FROM NEEDING IT [MT.15:21–28]

*[21] Next, Jesus traveled northwest into the region of Tyre and Sidon. [22] Imagine, a pagan woman from that area showed up and shouted, "Pity me, Lord, son of David. My daughter is troubled by a demon." [23] He gave no reply. The disciples told him, "Get rid of her. She'll keep yelling at us." [24] So he told her, "I've been sent to none but the lost sheep of the house of Israel." [25] But she came up, paid*

*him homage, and said, "Lord, help me."* [26] *He said, "It's not good to take the children's bread and toss it to the dogs."* [27] *"Yes, Lord," she said, "but dogs eat scraps that fall off the master's table."* [28] *"O, woman," he said, "your faith is great. Let it be as you desire." Her daughter was healed that hour.*

———🙣———

This scene is driven by a double dose of irony: a pagan woman teaches Jesus a lesson as she declares greater faith in God's healing power than has been expressed by many of Jesus' fellow Jews. Matthew doesn't say why Jesus traveled into this pagan territory, also called Syria [v.21]. But he told us earlier that people from there came to Jesus for healing (see 4:23). We can imagine him visiting these people—presumably Jews living in one of the many Jewish communities outside Israel. Whatever Jesus' purpose for visiting, it was impeded by a woman whose urgent pleas were so annoying that his disciples begged him to send her away [v.22–23].

Matthew says Jesus explained his inability to attend to her by trying to explain that, as a Jew—a son of David—he had to seek out fellow Jews who'd lost touch with the Covenant. This was also what he'd asked his disciples to do when he sent them out to teach and heal (see 10:5–6). As Matthew describes the situation, Jesus' task of remedial teaching of the Covenant didn't allow him time to bring the Good News to non-Jews [v.24]. But we hear that the woman's need made her deaf to this explanation of his mission, and she proclaimed her need baldly: "Help me!" [v.25].

According to Matthew, when the woman turned back on Jesus the image he'd used to define the limits of his mission, she helped him see things differently [vv.26–27]. Then we see Jesus doing what he'd been asking his disciples and others to do: he listened, and he learned. In this woman, Jesus again saw how faith in God's care could animate those who weren't officially included in God's Covenant (see 8:10). We hear him affirm the woman's trust in God and tell her it's God's deepest desire that we turn to him for all our needs [v.28]. It seems that, when we allow ourselves to recognize our desperation and then call out for help, as this woman does, we allow God to do what otherwise he cannot do: help.

## BACK HOME, JESUS HEADS UP THE MOUNTAIN AGAIN, AND TEACHES [MT.15:29–39]

*[29] Jesus returned to the Lake of Galilee. He went up to the heights for a while. [30] Great crowds came up. They brought him the feeble, the blind, the paralyzed, mutes, and others. He healed them. [31] People were amazed to see mutes speak, cripples able-bodied, the blind seeing, the feeble on their feet. They gave glory to the God of Israel. [32] Jesus gathered his disciples to say, "I feel pity for the crowd. They've been with me three days without food. I don't want to send them off hungry. They'll faint." [33] They asked, "Where can we get food for so many way out here?" [34] He asked in return, "How many loaves do you have?" "Seven—and a few fish," they said. [35] Jesus told the crowd to settle on the ground. [36] He took the seven loaves and the fish. He gave thanks. He broke them and gave them to the disciples to distribute. [37] Everyone ate and was satisfied. They gathered seven baskets of leftovers. [38] Four thousand men were fed—not counting women and children. [39] After sending the crowds away, he traveled by boat down the coast to Magadan.*

—◦◦◦—

Matthew has been casual in changing scenes (see 12:15) and time lines (see 14:12–13). Here [v.29], he describes Jesus—presumably returned to Capernaum from his trip north (see 15:21)—settled in on the heights, high above the lake (see 5:1). Matthew tells us that, in this instance, the needy crowds [v.30] attributed the healing they witnessed to "the God of Israel" [v.31]. This suggests they made a connection between the miraculous rehabilitations they saw and the care God promised to his people in the Covenant. Perhaps they felt close to the kingdom.

We next hear that days had passed and Jesus was concerned for the crowd's need for food [v.32]. It's clear from the response of his disciples that, despite the acts of healing they'd witnessed, plus Jesus' previous care for a hungry crowd (see 14:19–20), they didn't

feel close to God's kingdom [v.33]. They'd seen Jesus heal, and
they'd been sent to bring healing (see 10:8). Yet they still seem puzzled about God's power to care for our needs—especially when we
feel stymied by our sense of need [v.34]. According to Matthew,
once again Jesus demonstrated how God's care works (see 14:19).
First, relax [v.35]. Then, notice your situation, and give thanks to the
God who knows your needs better than you do. Finally, share
God's bountiful blessings [vv.36–37].

Matthew's narration says that, after being satisfied by God's care
and generosity, the crowds went home and Jesus continued to
travel—this time to Magadan, just south of Capernaum [vv.38–39].
Matthew doesn't mention a reason for Jesus' journey, but we can
assume it had the same purpose as the rest of his travels: continuing
to proclaim the presence of God's kingdom, and to invite people to
notice the benefits of accepting that kingdom as a divine gift.

# SIXTEEN

## Rejecting and Accepting
## Jesus' Message

NO ONE SEEMS TO UNDERSTAND JESUS'
MESSAGE OF REPENTANCE [MT.16:1–12]

*¹ Pharisees and Sadducees arrived [in Magadan (see 15:39)]. Trying to make a case, they asked him to produce a sign from heaven. ² He told them, "You say: 'Red sky in the evening: fair weather in the morning. ³ Red at morning: storms by evening.' You understand the sky, but not yourselves? ⁴ An evil, unfaithful age wants a sign but will get only the sign of Jonah." And he left. ⁵ When they left for the northeast shore of the lake, the disciples took no bread. ⁶ On the way, Jesus told them, "Beware the leaven of the Pharisees and Sadducees." ⁷ They said to one another, "He's talking about the lack of bread." ⁸ Jesus knew their concern. He said, "So little faith! Why do you talk about bread? ⁹ Don't you understand or remember the leftovers from five loaves for five thousand? ¹⁰ Do you remember the baskets of leftovers from seven loaves for four thousand? ¹¹ You think I'm speaking of bread? Beware the leaven of Pharisees and Sadducees!" ¹² Then they understood: he didn't mean the effect leaven has on bread, but the effect of the teaching from the Pharisees and Sadducees.*

―⁓◦⁓―

Pharisees and Sadducees, though not strictly Jewish officials, were influential opinion makers. Pharisees campaigned for a strict interpretation of scripture; Sadducees pushed for a stronger leadership of the priests. Here, Matthew describes some of them demanding that Jesus prove himself [v.1]—a demand that, like a previous one, received Jesus' offer of the same "sign" that Jonah offered (i.e., repentance; see 12:38–42). The irony is thick here as Matthew recounts Jesus' ridicule. Jonah offered only one sign to pagan Nineveh: God's call to repent. But now, in this age, these supposedly devout Jews understand the weather better than Jesus' call to repentance. We hear Jesus say that, if they believed in the offer made in the Covenant, they'd hear that offer anew in the proclamation of the Good News: repent, and turn to God's kingdom [vv.2–4].

Without ado, Matthew changes the scene [v.5]. But, before moving into new territory (see 16:13), Matthew says the disciples' confused response to a warning from Jesus provoked another lesson about faith in God's care [vv.6–8]. We hear Jesus remind them they saw him turn to the Father twice (see 14:19; 15:36) to address the need of hungry people [vv.9–10]. Though they'd seen this evidence of God's care for them, they still seemed anxious about their daily needs [v.11a]. Matthew says Jesus invited them to reflect now on what choice they needed to make in order to take in the right teaching: they could embrace the self-righteousness of the Pharisees, or they could notice their need for repentance [vv.11b–12].

## A GLIMMER OF ACCEPTANCE OF
## JESUS' MESSAGE [MT.16:13–20]

[13] *After arriving in the region of Caesarea-Philippi, he asked his disciples, "Who do people say the Son of Man is?"* [14] *"John the Baptist," some said. Others said, "Jeremiah"; or, "One of the prophets."* [15] *"And you," he said; "what do you say about me?"* [16] *Simon Peter said, "You're 'the Christ,' son of the living God."* [17] *"You're blessed, Simon, Jonah's son," said Jesus. "Flesh and blood didn't give you this revelation. My Father in heaven did.* [18] *And I say you are 'Peter'; you're the hard 'Rock' on which I'll build my church. The powers of the lower world*

*won't overwhelm it.* *¹⁹ To you I give the keys of the kingdom of heaven. What you bind on earth is already bound in heaven. What you let go on earth is already let go in heaven." ²⁰ Then he said very clearly that they shouldn't tell anyone he was "the Christ."*

—⟨ೲೲ⟩—

Matthew may have set this scene on the eastern side of the lake in order to picture the group away from crowds as Jesus unfolds a lesson very quickly and then asks the disciples to keep it to themselves. First, Matthew says the disciples responded to a question by saying their fellow Jews thought Jesus might turn out to be a special Son of Man—like the Baptist or one of the other great prophetic voices [vv.13–14]. Then he says they learned that one of them, Peter, believed Jesus was "the Messiah," God's "Anointed One" [v.15]—though we don't hear what Peter believed God had anointed Jesus to do. Next, we hear Jesus say that a clear sense of what God wants, chooses, or anoints for us can come only as a gift or blessing from God, and that Peter had just received such a blessing. Then we hear Jesus play with Peter's name to tell the disciples that the whole community of believers, his "church," would be made of people who, like Peter, allowed God to bless them with belief in Jesus' teaching, and that no power on earth was stronger than the bond of that blessing [v.18]. To give an idea of the power of believing, Matthew says Jesus used the image of keys, and of tying and untying: "Believing is the key into heaven. When belief in God directs your actions, you hold on to what heaven holds on to, and you let go of what heaven discards" [v.19].

Despite the simplicity and clarity of this lesson, Matthew portrays Jesus as unready to let the disciples speak to others about God's anointed one—"the Christ" [v.20]. If we wonder why Jesus had so little confidence in their ability to understand and share this lesson, we should read the next scene, in which we hear Jesus describe some of the things God has chosen for him—his anointed one—to experience.

JESUS' MESSAGE OF REPENTANCE
SEEMS BLEAK [MT.16:21–28]

*²¹ Jesus began to explain to his disciples that he had to go to Jerusalem; suffer under the elders, chief priests, and scribes; be killed; and be raised on the third day. ²² Peter took him aside to protest: "Heaven forbid, Lord. That can't happen to you!" ²³ Jesus turned on him, "Get behind me, Satan. You're trying to trip me up. You're thinking like a human, not like God." ²⁴ Jesus told the disciples, "If you want to follow me, turn away from yourself. Take up your cross, and follow me. ²⁵ Those who want to save themselves will get lost. Those who let go of their lives for my sake will find life. ²⁶ Would you trade your soul even for the whole world? What can replace your soul? ²⁷ The Son of Man will come with the glory of his Father and his angels to give each person whatever their deeds demand. ²⁸ O yes, indeed, I say some of you here won't taste death until you see the Son of Man coming in his kingdom."*

———

Matthew here reports that, after Jesus told his disciples not to speak about his identity as the Christ (see just above), he told them his mission would lead to opposition, suffering, and death—but would also lead to his resurrection [v.21]. And he tells us Jesus responded to Peter's attempt to correct him [v.22] by speaking to him as he had once spoken to the devil (see 4:9–10): he says he chooses God's way of seeing our needs, not the human way of reacting to them [v.23]. Jesus' candid words here about struggling against temptation suggest how much work it takes to keep believing in God's plan for our lives, while Peter's protest indicates how easy it is to want a different plan.

Then we see Jesus reminding the disciples that, if they choose to learn from him, they must bear the burden, or cross, of facing life as he does: with trust in God rather than themselves [v.24]. Refraining from making a desperate grab at life will, paradoxically, get them what they seek: life [v.25]. As Jesus describes it, turning to God is a simple and obvious choice: choose to be fulfilled by God's life, or choose nothingness [v.26].

As the scene nears an end, we hear a warning: If you behave as one who has accepted God's Covenant, you'll be considered, or judged, as God's partner. But if you have turned your back on that relationship, your actions will be judged accordingly [v.27]. Matthew closes the scene by describing Jesus telling those around him that, if they live a bit longer, they'll witness the power of the kingdom—that is, his return from death in the resurrection [v.28]. He's telling them God's promise of divine life, repeated throughout the story told in scripture, is true. Do they want to accept that promise?

# SEVENTEEN
## Lessons in Trusting

### DIVINE GLORY DOESN'T LOOK LIKE
### HUMAN GLORY [MT.17:1–13]

*¹ Six days later, Jesus took just Peter, James, and his brother, John, to a high mountain. ² He was transfigured in front of them—his face like the sun, his clothes like light. ³ Imagine, Moses and Elijah also appeared, talking with Jesus. ⁴ Peter's response was: "Lord, it's good we're here. If you'd like, I can make three tents—for you, for Moses, and for Elijah." ⁵ Imagine, as he spoke, a dazzling cloud settled on them. A voice spoke from the cloud: "This is my beloved Son. I am deeply pleased with him. Listen to him." ⁶ When the disciples heard this, they fell flat, terrified. ⁷ Jesus came over, touched them, and said, "Get up. Don't be afraid." ⁸ When they looked up, they saw only Jesus. ⁹ As they descended, Jesus said, "Don't speak of this vision until the Son of Man is raised from the dead." ¹⁰ The disciples then asked why the scribes maintained that, first, Elijah had to come. ¹¹ "Elijah is indeed to come and reconcile all," he said. ¹² "And I say Elijah's already come. But, instead of accepting him, they did what they wanted with him—a fate that awaits the Son of Man." ¹³ The disciples realized he was talking about John the Baptist.*

———

Matthew says that, without explanation, Jesus gave three disciples an experience of divine glory—a dazzling vision of an intimate conversation [vv.1–3]. He describes Peter's response as so bedazzled that, rather than savoring or entering the conversation, he was eager to contain the splendor of the moment in tents [v.4]. He seems like the proud parent who fumbles around in search of the cell phone or camera while the child pipes its first word—thus missing what's actually happening. Then we hear Peter being corrected by the Father's voice: "Listen!" Matthew is making the point that there's no need to build a special place for the divine presence because God speaks to us directly—through the prophets, for instance, and now through his Son. All we need to do is listen. But Matthew depicts the disciples being terrified by God's voice, then comforted by Jesus [vv.5–8]. Perhaps because the disciples hadn't understood their experience, Jesus asked them not to share it yet [v.9].

Next we see the disciples asking how Elijah's return would herald a triumphant, glorious Day of the Lord (see Mal.3:23). Matthew describes them as being as puzzled and unsure about this promised revelation of glory as Peter had been of his recent experience of God's glory. And he shows us Jesus challenging them to imagine God's glory working in ways that might seem the opposite of earthly magnificence. For example, could the fate John suffered also await Jesus? If so, could they imagine God's glory being revealed in that fate [vv.10–13]?

## DIVINE POWER IS UNLIKE HUMAN POWER [MT.17:14–27]

*14 As they came down the mountain, they met a crowd. One man came up and knelt. 15 "Lord," he said, "have pity on my son. He has painful seizures, falling into the fire or into water. 16 I brought him to your disciples, but they couldn't heal him." 17 "O, what a faithless generation," said Jesus. "How long am I with you; how can I take it? Bring him here." 18 Jesus gave the demon an order, and it left. The boy was immediately healed. 19 When Jesus and the disciples were alone, they asked, "Why couldn't we expel it?" 20 "Because of your little faith," he said. "O yes, indeed, I say, if your faith was the size of a mustard seed, but you said to this mountain, 'Move,' it would move. For nothing's impossible." [²¹ Scholars say words about prayer and fasting were added later.] ²² As they headed to Galilee, Jesus said, "The Son of Man will be put in men's hands. ²³ They'll kill him. And he'll be raised on the third day." They were very sad. ²⁴ At Capernaum, Temple-tax collectors asked Peter, "Does your teacher pay the tax?" ²⁵ "Yes," he said. When he got home, Jesus spoke up, "What do you think, Simon: do earthly kings take taxes and tariffs from sons of the realm, or from aliens?" ²⁶ "From aliens," said Peter. "Then the sons are exempt," said Jesus. ²⁷ "But, let's not upset them. Go drop a hook in the lake. Open the mouth of the first fish you catch. You'll find a coin. It'll cover the Temple tax for both of us."*

Matthew here combines a flurry of activity with a mix of moods. He depicts Jesus and three disciples rejoining the others (see 17:1) in the middle of a scene of failed healing [vv.14–16]. Jesus' reaction is like a teacher's bewilderment after a simple lesson hasn't sunk in: "If someone is bedeviled or unwell, to whom should they turn?" [vv.17–18]. Matthew says that, when the disciples asked, in effect, "What did we do wrong?" [v.19], Jesus had to tell them yet again to trust in God, not themselves. They don't have the power to move mountains or make all things possible, but because God does have that power, they needn't waste time trying to master the universe. They can turn to God when their needs are greater than their powers [v.20].

Then Matthew depicts Jesus and his disciples on the move again, traveling in Galilee. He tells us Jesus once more told them that, after his defeat by the authorities, he'd be raised to life (see 16:21). According to Matthew, the disciples heard only the first, disheartening part of Jesus' words [vv.22–23]. Without comment on this sadness, Matthew suddenly describes a serious objection from some collectors of the Temple tax, and a humorous response. He shows us Jesus portraying tax collecting as part of the coercive power of worldly authority, then noting that the children of God needed no coercion to support one another in their attempts to give thanks and worship to their Father [vv.25–26]. But, Jesus seems to say, one can fish out a coin as easily as pull up a hook. So, rather than debate the manner of collecting money for the Temple, pay the tax [v.27].

# EIGHTEEN

## Divine Power Is Seen in Humility, Patience, and Forgiveness

WHAT IT MEANS TO BE LOWLY AND WEAK [MT.18:1–9]

*¹ [After they returned to Capernaum,] Jesus' disciples asked him, "Who's the greatest in the kingdom of heaven?" ² He called a child into the group. ³ "Ah yes, indeed, I tell you that, unless you change and become like children, you won't enter the kingdom of heaven. ⁴ If you make yourself as lowly as this child, you'll be the greatest in the kingdom. ⁵ If you accept someone as lowly as this one, you accept me. ⁶ Whoever trips up a little one who believes in me, well, better for them to go into the sea with a millstone around the neck. ⁷ You who trip up others, beware! O, people will fall, but woe to you who push them. ⁸ If your hand or foot makes you fall, cut it off and throw it away. Better to come to life disabled or lame than be thrown with all limbs into an unquenchable fire. ⁹ If your eye leads you astray, pluck it out and throw it away. Better to come to life one-eyed than take two eyes to Gehenna—the place of unquenchable flame."*

———∽∾∽———

We can picture the disciples and Jesus still in Galilee (see 17:22), where, as Matthew tells it, lessons continued [v.1], with Jesus suggesting that, if the disciples wanted to imagine what the kingdom of heaven was like, they should start with the image of a child. For only children are admitted to this kingdom [vv.2–3]. According to Matthew's description of Jesus' teaching, the more lowly and dependent you are, the higher your place in God's kingdom—the purpose of which is care of the needy [v.4]. And, if you'd like to experience the heavenly kingdom as Jesus does, simply welcome one of the lowly ones into your care [v.5].

However, if you despise those who are weak and lowly, or if you hinder them from reaching out to God in their desperation, you'll discover what it's like to feel fathomless despair. Yes, some desperate people might lose hope, but those who provoke or encourage their desperation will never be able to share God's life [vv.6–7]. Matthew describes Jesus using images of abandoning parts of your body as you head toward eternal life rather than allowing them to lead you to fall away from trust in God. Is there something that leads you to mistrust God? Abandon it. Are you madly attached to something that has nothing to do with God? Let it go. Your blind attachment will not satisfy you. It can, however, consume you with an endlessly galling sense of loss and wasted opportunity. That would be like winding up permanently in a perpetually smoldering dump, that is, Gehenna [vv.8–9].

## PATIENCE AND FORGIVENESS ARE
## DIVINE WORK [MT.18:10–20]

*10 Jesus continued to speak about the lowly: "Don't despise the lowly. Listen, their angels gaze constantly on my Father's face in heaven. [11 This verse about the Son of Man saving the lost is regarded as a late addition.] 12 What do you think—if one from a flock of a hundred sheep wandered off, wouldn't the shepherd leave the ninety-nine on the slopes and look for the stray? 13 And if he finds it, O yes, indeed, I tell you he'll cherish it more than the nonstrays. 14 Your Father in heaven doesn't want to lose the least lowly one. 15 If your brother sins, correct him privately. If he listens, you've brought a brother back to you. 16 If he doesn't listen, call in two or three witnesses to listen, then report what they heard. 17 If he won't listen to them, tell the whole church. If he won't listen to them, let that one be treated as you would a Gentile or tax collector. 18 O yes, indeed, I tell you what you bind on earth is bound in heaven; what you let go on earth is let go by heaven. [19] O yes, I say if two of you on earth pray together for something, the Father will do it. [20] For, where two or three assemble in my name, I'm there in their midst."*

———*◊◊◊*———

Matthew describes Jesus explaining the process of allowing God to raise us up from lowliness. He asks us to imagine angels whose constant work is to look into God's face for those who can't yet do it themselves [v.10], and to imagine that the Father is as determined to bring his children into his eternal presence as a shepherd is intent to keep his flock safe [vv.12–14].

Then Matthew describes Jesus explaining how to imitate God's work of reconciliation. The lesson might be summarized as follows. If you are offended by someone, speak to them about it. Who knows, you may get the reaction: "I hadn't noticed! Forgive me!" Rejoice [v.15]. However, if your fellow believer won't discuss an offense, ask for help in the discussion [v.16]. If that doesn't lead to reconciliation, get help from the whole community of believers— the church. If the person refuses to reconcile with the community, "that one" is now outside the community [v.17]. This would leave the person where Jesus finds all of us: in the position of a sinner who needs to hear the Good News of repentance. (Who might be called upon to answer that need?)

Matthew then describes Jesus giving all believers the power he gave Peter (see 16:19): to be moved by the example, inspiration, and blessing of God in binding up, healing, and uniting one another as his children, as well as freeing others from hurt, anger, and dismay through reconciliation and forgiveness [v.18]. We hear Jesus say, "Yes, if two of you long for the divine gift of reconciliation and forgiveness, just ask for it [v.19]; yes, as you share my work of turning to the Father, I continue to work in you" [v.20].

## WE ARE CALLED TO SHARE THE DIVINE WORK
## OF FORGIVENESS [MT.18:21–35]

*²¹ Peter asked, "Lord, how many times must I forgive a brother who hurts me— seven?" ²² "No," said Jesus, "not as many as seven—as many as seven times seven! ²³ Listen, the kingdom of heaven is like a king asking servants for loan repayments. ²⁴ One debtor was ushered in owing ten thousand talents, a huge sum. ²⁵ For payment, the king ordered him sold, along with wife, children, and goods. ²⁶ The desperate servant fell down and begged, 'Be patient, and I'll pay it all.' ²⁷ Moved with pity, the king pardoned the servant and forgave the debt. ²⁸ When that one left, he saw a fellow servant who owed him a small amount. He grabbed him by the neck and demanded, 'Pay me your debt.' ²⁹ That servant fell down and begged, 'Be patient, and I'll repay you.' ³⁰ He wouldn't agree. He had him imprisoned until he could pay. ³¹ When fellow servants saw this, they were shocked. They told the king about it. ³² The king shouted: 'You wicked slave. I forgave your whole debt when you begged for time to pay it. ³³ Shouldn't you have shown mercy to your fellow servant, as I had mercy on you?' ³⁴ The angry king handed him over to torturers until he paid everything. ³⁵ That's what my Father in heaven will do to you unless you forgive from the heart."*

According to Matthew, Peter wanted to put a limit on forgiveness: after suffering seven personal offenses, should the aggrieved party have to forgive further? No, we hear Jesus say, there isn't any limit to forgiveness if we're learning it from God [vv.21–22]. To make this point, Matthew says Jesus told a story. The Lord in the story has absolute power. He's free to set down the law for those who serve him—even to sell them out of his realm [vv.23–25]. But this tyrant is obviously not an ogre. In fact, he's easily moved by the pleas of a servant in a hopeless situation, and he accepts a huge loss in order to free the man from woe [vv.26–27].

Surprisingly, the servant who was blessed with forgiveness shows no sign of wanting to share that blessing, even when he's begged to do so [vv.28–30]. Like this man's fellow servants, we too may be shocked at his demand of jail time for so small a debt; and we may feel relieved when the king is alerted [v.31]. We may also sympathize with the king's surprise and anger that the forgiven servant would be so unmoved by the pardon of his huge debt that he had no impulse to share the delights of mercy and forgiveness [vv.32–33]. What a horrifying conclusion to this story: endless agony, and no forgiveness in sight [v.34].

Jesus' story leaves all who accept the Covenant a clear choice. We can delight in God's pardon of our selfishness by sharing the joy of forgiveness with others. Or, seeking self-righteousness, we can remain unforgiven, clinging only to our grudges [v.35].

# NINETEEN

## On the Way to Jerusalem:
## Meeting Challenges; Teaching

### MORE CHALLENGES [MT.19:1–12]

*¹ Jesus left Galilee and traveled south to Judea, on the west bank of the Jordan. ² Great crowds followed him there, and he cured them. ³ Pharisees popped up with another test. They asked, "May a man divorce his wife for any reason?" ⁴ He asked, "Haven't you read that, in the beginning, the Creator made them male and female? ⁵ That's why a man leaves mother and father and joins his wife—two as one flesh. ⁶ They're no longer two; they're one flesh. What God joins, humans don't divide." ⁷ "Then why," they asked, "did Moses say to give a certificate for a divorce?" ⁸ He said, "Moses allowed divorce because of hard hearts. In the beginning, it wasn't so. ⁹ And I say one who divorces a lawful wife to marry another is adulterous." ¹⁰ His disciples said, "If that's true, it's better not to marry." ¹¹ He said, "People won't understand this unless they see it as a gift. ¹² Look, some people are born eunuchs; some are castrated; some choose celibacy because of the kingdom of God. If you can make that choice, good."*

—⟨෴⟩—

In Matthew's narration, this is Jesus' first trip to Judea, where he's portrayed healing [vv.1–2] and being pestered by Pharisees [v.3]. At this point, it shouldn't surprise us when Matthew says Jesus told his

inquisitors to recall scripture—to remember that God, who wants
us to accept his Covenant, began creation not by making isolated
individuals but by fashioning them in a relationship [vv.4–5]. Since
God wants to unite us, we shouldn't split us up [v.6].

Matthew doesn't show us Jesus addressing the Pharisees' distortion of the Law—which describes a bill of divorce as an admission
of human inability to keep the commitment (see Dt.24:1–4)—but
noting that, from the beginning, God called us to trust him to bind
up and heal what we see as broken. If we don't trust him to do that
work satisfactorily—if, say, we create and break a relationship of
marriage simply to satisfy ourselves—we will be abusing God's
creation [vv.7–9]. In answer to the disciples' description of God's
notion of marriage as impossible [v.10], Jesus describes various
ways to respond to God's decision to create marriage as an image of
himself (see Gn.1:27). Some people won't accept the possibility that
two individuals can be given the gift of becoming one [v.11]. Others
are born physically or mentally incapable of sharing the intimate
union of marriage; still others become incapable of it; and some, in
witness to the union that will one day bind us all in the kingdom,
live as celibates to remind us that this communion isn't created by
us, but by God [v.12a]. Matthew says Jesus concluded with the
simple advice that one should accept whichever form of witness
one feels capable of accepting [v.12b].

## JESUS REVIEWS HIS BASIC TEACHING [MT.19:13–30]

*13 When they brought children up for Jesus' touch and prayers, the disciples
objected. 14 But he said, "Let the children come to me; don't stop them. The
kingdom's for them." 15 He rested his hands on them, and moved on. 16 A man
came up, asking, "Teacher, what good must I do to have eternal life?" 17 Jesus
said, "Good? It's good to keep the commandments." 18 "Which?" Jesus said,
"These: 'You shall not kill, commit adultery, steal, or bear false witness. 19 You
shall honor your father and mother, and love your neighbor as yourself.'" 20 The
young man said, "I've kept all these. What else do I need?" 21 "If you want
fulfillment," said Jesus, "Sell all you have; give the money to the poor; let your*

*treasure be only heaven; then, come follow me."* [22] *When the young man heard this he went away dejected. He had many possessions.* [23] *"O yes, indeed, I say it's hard for the rich to enter the kingdom of heaven.* [24] *O, yes, a camel gets through a needle's eye easier than the rich get into the kingdom."* [25] *His disciples were astonished and asked, "Who, then, can be saved?"* [26] *He stared at them: "It's impossible for humans, but for God nothing's impossible!"* [27] *Peter said, "Look, we've left all to follow you. What will be for us?"* [28] *"O yes, indeed, to my followers I say: in the new age, when the Son of Man sits on the throne of glory, you'll sit on twelve thrones judging the twelve tribes of Israel.* [29] *Those who gave up home—parents, siblings, children, goods—for me, will get much more: eternal life!* [30] *But many who are 'first' will be last. The 'last' will be first."*

Matthew here shows Jesus reviewing essential lessons. First, those who feel a need for the kingdom are like children; they have no sense of power [vv.13–14]. Second, those who accept God's Covenant, follow God's commands, and yearn to share God's presence more intimately [vv.16–20], should forget about everything but following Jesus [v.21]—whose mission is to proclaim the richness of repentance. Matthew describes Jesus saying that this mission won't attract those who feel bound to other riches [v.22]. This point is stressed when Jesus repeats it, offering the image of an impossibly constrained camel [vv.23–24].

Matthew says these lessons made no sense to the disciples [v.25], and that Jesus' patient response to them was to remind them of the Covenant: God says, "I'm your God, you're my people; I make all things possible for you—not the other way around" [v.26]. According to Matthew, Peter's response to this reminder that God cares for them was to ask what reward the disciples would get in return for following Jesus [v.27]. Jesus then asks Peter to imagine sharing with him God's glory and power [v.28]—a power in which the children of God (the twelve tribes) did not always believe. Can Peter and other disciples imagine finding eternal life if they stop clinging to the prizes, possessions, and rewards of this life [v.29]? The lesson ends with a warning: Don't think you can earn God's power and glory as a reward for something you've done. Such gifts can be accepted—as gifts—only by those who are the last to imagine that they could possibly deserve them [v.30].

# TWENTY

## Reviewing Lessons about the Kingdom, Suffering, Greatness, and Healing

### WHAT'S THE KINGDOM LIKE? [MT.20:1–16]

*¹ Jesus continued teaching: "The kingdom of heaven is like the master of an estate going out first thing in the morning to hire workers for his vineyard. ² They agreed on a denarius—the daily wage—and he sent them into his vineyard. ³ Three hours later, he saw others in the market place without work. ⁴ He said, 'If you also go to my vineyard, I'll pay what's right.' ⁵ So, they went. He went back at the sixth and ninth hour and said the same. ⁶ Returning at the eleventh hour, he found others: 'Why are you here all day, idle?' ⁷ 'Because no one hired us,' they said. He said, 'You go into my vineyard too.' ⁸ At sundown, he told the foreman to pay the workers: last, first; first-hired, last. ⁹ Those hired at the eleventh hour came up and received a denarius. ¹⁰ When the first-hired came up, they thought they'd get more. They got a denarius. ¹¹ When they got it, they muttered about the estate-holder. ¹² 'You treat these late-comers, working one hour, the same as us, who bore the day's heat.' ¹³ 'Sir,' he said, 'I do you no wrong. Didn't we agree on a denarius? ¹⁴ Accept what's yours, and go. I want to give these last what I gave you. ¹⁵ Can't I use what I have as I want—or, do you cast an envious eye on my goodness?' ¹⁶ And that," said Jesus, "is how the 'first' will be last, and the 'last' will be first."*

———— *◦◦◦◦* ————

Matthew told us Jesus traveled into Judea (see 19:1)—presumably toward Jerusalem. His description of Jesus on this journey is similar to others: Jesus teaches and heals, repeating certain basic lessons. In this scene, we hear Jesus tell another parable about the kingdom: a landowner, finding more and more people available for work, promises to pay whatever's fair to those who are hired [vv.1–7]; and it turns out that his idea of "right," "just," and "fair" is to pay each laborer the same wage [vv.8–10].

I find it easy to echo the aggrieved response of the all-day worker [vv.11–12]—even after the employer explains the justice of his actions [vv.13–15]. But, if I plead, "Shouldn't you be generous to me too," the parable's lesson leaps at me: I'm assuming I can earn generosity; I can become entitled to it. In this story, all the workers needed the work, and they all had the good fortune to be hired. Nonetheless, the story says, some felt envious that the need for a full day's wage—a need shared by each of the workers—was recognized and met by the landowner. How easy it is to imagine that I've worked for my good fortune; to think that, when blessings are bestowed for effort, I should be at the head of the line. How unappealing to be needy, to have no boasts, to be last. But it's only the needy who cry out for help. And God hears their cry first [v.16].

## SUFFERING, SERVING, AND HEALING [MT.20:17–34]

[17] *On the way to Jerusalem, Jesus spoke to the twelve privately.* [18] *"Look, we're going up to Jerusalem. The Son of Man will be handed to the chief priests and scribes, who will condemn him to death.* [19] *They'll give him to Gentiles to mock, whip, and crucify. The third day, he'll rise."* [20] *The mother of Zebedee's sons came up with them to bow and ask a favor.* [21] *"Yes?" She said, "Arrange for my sons to sit left and right of you in the kingdom."* [22] *"You don't know what you ask," said Jesus. "Can you drink the cup I'll drink?" "Yes," they said.* [23] *"Yes, you'll drink the cup. But sitting right or left is for the Father to give, not me."* [24] *The ten were angry when they heard about the brothers.* [25] *But Jesus got them together. "You know Gentile rulers are lordly, willful tyrants.* [26] *Not so with you. If*

*you want to be great in this group, become the group's servant. ²⁷ If you want to be the first in the group, become the group's slave. ²⁸ The Son of Man didn't come to be served, but to serve—to give his life for others." ²⁹ As they moved through Jericho, a large crowd followed him. ³⁰ Two blind men sitting by the road cried as Jesus passed, "Mercy, Son of David!" ³¹ When the crowd told them to be quiet, they cried louder, "Mercy, Son of David!" ³² Jesus stopped, called them, and asked, "What do you want me to do?" ³³ "Lord, let our eyes be opened." ³⁴ Jesus, moved with pity, touched their eyes. They saw. They followed him.*

Here we read a reminder (see 16:21; 17:23) of what the future holds [vv.17–19], then a description of some secret dealing [vv.20–21]. Matthew says Jesus turned the brothers' special pleading into a basic question about repentance: were they ready to let God shape their future? If so, they had to follow Jesus' example and leave their ultimate destiny to God [vv.22–23].

After reporting fits of indignation [v.24], Matthew repeats a lesson that describes how God's kingdom of love differs from the world's fractiousness: because God cares for all his children, all his children will care for one another—indeed, they'll serve one another. If we need an example of what this service looks like, we can look to Jesus [vv.25–28]. Matthew then offers an example of service. As Jesus gets closer to Jerusalem, crowds gather [v.29], but disapprove of the noisy pleas of two desperate blind men [vv.30–31]. Matthew doesn't say why the crowd wanted no attention paid to these men, but he does describe Jesus' opposite reaction: he wanted to listen to their need [v.32]; and the men are happy to tell him about it [v.33].

Here, as we see Jesus approaching Jerusalem, it would be natural to suppose he might have been anxious about his future, discouraged by his failure to persuade Jewish leaders to listen to him, and exhausted by the disputatious slowness of his disciples. But Matthew continues to describe him as he has from the beginning of his Gospel: a believer and teacher of the Good News who was responsive to the needs of others [v.34].

# TWENTY-ONE
## First Days in Jerusalem

### ACCLAIM; INDIGNATION [MT.21:1–17]

*¹ When they got to the Mount of Olives, east of Jerusalem, near Bethphage, Jesus sent off two disciples. ² "In this village of Bethphage," he said, "you'll see an ass and its colt tied up. Bring them to me. ³ If someone questions you, say, 'The Lord needs them'; he'll send them right away." ⁴ This showed how fully the prophet spoke the truth [see Is.62:11; Zec.9:9]: ⁵ "Tell Zion's daughter, 'Look, your king comes on lowly mounts, an ass and a colt." ⁶ The disciples did what Jesus asked them to do. ⁷ They brought the donkey and colt. They put cloaks on them. He took his seat. ⁸ A large crowd put cloaks on the road. Some cut branches to put on the road. ⁹ In front and behind, they cried, "Hosanna [i.e., Save us!], Son of David." "Blessed is the one who comes in the Lord's name" [Ps.118:26]. "Lord in high heaven, save us!" ¹⁰ When he entered Jerusalem, the whole city wondered: "Who's this?" ¹¹ Some answered, "This is the prophet, Jesus, from Nazareth in Galilee." ¹² Jesus went to the Temple and threw out the merchants—knocking over the money changers' tables and the stools of the dove sellers. ¹³ "It's written: 'My house is a house of prayer' [Is.56:7]. You make it a bandit cave!" ¹⁴ The blind and the lame came up to him in the Temple. He healed them. ¹⁵ But priests and scribes were angered by all this, and by hearing children cry, "Hosanna." ¹⁶ "Don't you hear?" they complained. He said, "Did you read, 'He brings praise from infant lips'?" ¹⁷ He left them and the city, and spent the night at Bethany, near Bethphage.*

—————

Matthew's description of Jesus' instructions suggests he'd made careful preparations to demonstrate what sort of king the prophets had told people to expect—that is, a king that did not announce his presence with regal pomp, but with simplicity [vv.1–5]. However, Matthew's description of people's cries for salvation leaves us doubting they understood the lesson that salvation comes quietly. They seem to hope Jesus will be another David, a powerful ruler [vv.6–9]. The crowds in Jerusalem are said to be puzzled by Jesus' arrival [v.10], despite the fact that some knew his reputation as a prophet [v.11].

Then Matthew tells us Jesus gave all in the Temple a demonstration of the need for repentance: the merchants there needed to turn away from their fixation on business and turn, instead, to God [vv.12–13]. After this confrontation, Matthew depicts a roiling scene: crowds press for cures; children repeat the cry of "Save us"; and officials complain about the hubbub and hosannas. He says Jesus asked the disgruntled priests and scribes to recall a promise they'd surely read in scripture (see Ps.8:2): God can inspire praise in unlikely ways from unlikely people [vv.14–16]. We don't hear how these officials responded to this not-so-subtle call to repent and hear God's word. Matthew says Jesus left them with their thoughts for the night [v.17].

## JESUS TEACHES AGAIN ABOUT FAITH
## AND REPENTANCE [MT.21:18–32]

*[18] Returning to the city early the next morning, Jesus was hungry. [19] Stopping at a fruitless fig tree, he said, "Never bear fruit again." It died. [20] The disciples were amazed: "How did the fig tree wither up so quickly?" [21] "O yes, indeed, I say if you have faith, not doubt, you'll do more than this; you'll say to this mountain [on which Jerusalem sits], 'Up! Into the sea!' and it will happen. [22] Whatever you pray for as believers, you'll receive." [23] In the Temple, priests and elders stopped him: "By whose authority do you teach?" [24] "Answer a question," he said, "then I'll tell*

*you by whose authority I do what I do. <sup>25</sup> Was John's baptism of God, or humans?" They thought if they said, "God," he'd say, "Then why didn't you believe him?" <sup>26</sup> But they feared the crowd if they said, "human," for the crowd saw John as a prophet. <sup>27</sup> They said, "We don't know." He said, "Then I won't say on whose authority I act. <sup>28</sup> Now, think about this: a man tells his first son to work in the vineyard. <sup>29</sup> He says, 'No. I don't want to.' But later, he changes his mind, and he goes. <sup>30</sup> The man tells a second son the same thing. He says, 'Yes, sir,' but he doesn't go. <sup>31</sup> Who did the father's will?" "The first," they said. "O yes, indeed, I say tax collectors and prostitutes go ahead of you into God's kingdom. <sup>32</sup> When John showed the right way, you didn't believe; tax collectors and prostitutes did. But, even with their witness, you didn't believe."*

In this section, Matthew depicts three teaching moments. In the first, he shows Jesus using a tree as a prop to remind the disciples that God, who knows all needs, always responds to prayers that ask for greater faith: "If you needed a mountain to move, to whom would you turn for the power to believe you could move it?" [vv.18–22]. He describes a second lesson as the result of Jesus being provoked by officials who trusted their own judgment so strongly that, even after Jesus had helped them see they couldn't trust their judgment, they seemed unmoved by his invitation to let go of their delusional self-confidence [vv.23–27].

As Matthew describes it, Jesus, undaunted by this failure to enlighten his adversaries, began a third moment of teaching in which we hear another story or parable about the kingdom. It makes the obvious point that someone who cares about the wishes of another will learn to share those wishes even if, at first, there is a reluctance to do so. In other words, to repair a relationship, one needs to change the choice that damaged the relationship [vv.28–31a].

These lessons are summed up by Matthew with Jesus' recollections about crafty tax collectors and worldly-wise prostitutes who realized their confidence had been misplaced. They therefore gave up faith in themselves, and they turned to God. Matthew depicts Jesus commenting sadly on the fact that their witness of placing trust in God apparently didn't encourage the priests and elders to hear the Good News about repentance [vv.31b–32].

## JESUS TEACHES ABOUT JUDGMENT [MT.21:33–46]

*[33] Jesus told another parable: "A man planted a vineyard, fenced it, put in a wine press and a watch tower, then leased it and moved away. [34] At harvest time, he sent servants to collect his share. [35] The tenants took the servants and beat one, killed another, and stoned a third. [36] He then sent a larger delegation of servants, but the tenants treated them the same. [37] At last he sent his son, thinking, 'They'll respect my son.' [38] But, the tenants said, 'This is the heir. Kill him, and the inheritance is ours!' [39] They threw him out of the vineyard and killed him. [40] When the owner himself comes, what will he do to the tenants?" [41] They said, "He'll give those evil men an evil end, and lease to trustworthy tenants." [42] "Have you read in scripture: 'The stone rejected by the builders becomes the corner stone. The Lord did this. Isn't that wonderful!' [Ps.18:22–23]? [43] The kingdom will be taken from you and given to those who will find it fruitful." [[44] A comment about being destroyed by a stone is missing in most manuscripts.] [45] The chief priests and Pharisees realized the parables were about them. [46] They wanted to arrest him but feared to do so, for the crowds saw him as a prophet.*

We can listen to this parable as though it's addressed only to the Jewish officials who've questioned Jesus' right to teach (see 21:23). Matthew even tells us the officials made this assumption [v.45]. It's easy not only to see that the tenants' behavior is foolish [vv.33–39], but also to see how the officials are like them, and it's chilling to hear the officials say they understand the fate of double-dealers who break a deal. For they are double-dealers when they put trust in themselves rather than the God who made a Covenant with them—in effect, killing their relationship with God [vv.40–41].

Any pleasure we take in judging the hectoring officials may be spoiled by the question addressed to them about the psalm describing God's habit of doing the unexpected [v.42]. Perhaps we don't find it wonderful that God surprises us and challenges our prejudices. But, according to Matthew, Jesus said that only those who learned to rejoice in God's unpredictable way of shaping life would be ready to enjoy God's kingdom. And those who refused to learn this lesson would never enjoy the kingdom [v.43].

Matthew gives us a hint of what keeps the officials from being able to learn, to repent, or to hear the Good News. As he reports in Jesus' description of them, they're obsessed by public opinion and by the power they have to shape that opinion [vv.45–46]. It seems that, if they feel certain they already know how life should be shaped, no parable about repentance and a change of heart can possibly sound like Good News to them.

# TWENTY-TWO

## In Jerusalem, Jesus Continues Proclaiming Good News

### GOOD NEWS FOR THOSE WHO SEEK THE KINGDOM [MT.22:1–14]

*¹ Still teaching in the Temple, Jesus told another parable: ² "The kingdom of heaven is like a king who prepared a wedding feast for his son. ³ He sent servants to call the invited to the banquet, but they didn't want to come. ⁴ He instructed other servants, 'Tell the invited, "Look, my fattened cattle are slaughtered and everything's prepared. Come to the banquet."' ⁵ But they paid no attention. One went off to his estate, another to his business. ⁶ Others grabbed the servants, then tortured and killed them. ⁷ The furious king sent troops to wipe out the murderers and burn their cities. ⁸ Then he said to his servants, 'The wedding feast's ready, but the invited wouldn't come. ⁹ Go now to the crossroads and invite whoever you encounter.' ¹⁰ The servants invited everyone on the road—good and bad—until the feast was full. ¹¹ The king entered and saw a man reclining at table without a wedding garment. ¹² 'Friend,' he said, 'why aren't you wearing a wedding garment?' He said nothing. ¹³ He told his servants, 'Throw him, bound, into the dark to weep and gnash his teeth.'" ¹⁴ Then Jesus said, "Many are called, but few are chosen."*

⎯⎯⎯✸⎯⎯⎯

If we imagine Jesus addressing the officials who've been resisting his teaching [see 21:45], we may think this parable is aimed only at them. Like the parable about bone-headed tenants [see 21:33–41], it describes extremely foolish and shockingly violent actions. Few who hear this story will say, "I can see myself doing that." And few will find it difficult to sympathize with the king's decision to punish such behavior [vv.1–7].

But it may surprise us that the king in the story isn't disheartened by the rudeness of those who spurned his invitation. He wants a feast, so he seeks anyone who'll accept an invitation. And he gets his wish. His hall is filled with festive diners [vv.8–10]. So, why the fuss about one improperly dressed guest? Well, suppose you hear that your whole town's been invited to a party, and you arrive to find that the party is actually a wedding feast. Should you go home to dress properly for the occasion? The man in the story can't answer that question [vv.11–12]. The invitation to the feast doesn't seem as important to him as it is to the king. If we're like that man— if we don't accept God's invitation as he defines it—we'll have no reason to stay at the feast. Matthew tells us that Jesus said people will groan their regrets with grimaces on their faces if they don't take God's invitation to his kingdom seriously [v.13]. The last words of this lesson, "few are chosen," remind us that it's not enough for God to invite us into his kingdom. We must choose to respond—a choice that he will affirm, making us "chosen" [v.14].

### JESUS TURNS A TRAP INTO A LESSON [MT.22:15–22]

*15 The Pharisees left the Temple to plan how to catch Jesus in an error. 16 They sent their disciples and some staunch supporters of King Herod to say, "Teacher, we know you're honest, teaching God's way truly. You're not concerned with opinion or prestige. 17 So, what do you think is right: can we pay a tax to Caesar, or not?" 18 Jesus saw their ill will. "What fakers," he said. "Why try to trick me? 19 Show me the coin that pays the tax." They gave him a denarius. 20 "Whose head's this, and whose title?" he asked. 21 "The emperor's," they said. "Give*

*Caesar's things to Caesar. Give God's things to God," he said.* [22] *Dumbfounded, they left.*

Matthew has repeatedly depicted Jesus as a man whose words and actions proclaim a deep belief in the Covenant, God's promise to care for his people. In his teaching, Jesus has described the joy of repenting, turning away from all other blandishments, and putting one's trust in God. In his acts of healing, Jesus has demonstrated his faith that God is fulfilling the plan he initiated at creation: to share divine life with us humans. Jesus' faith will soon be tested as he faces death, but, according to Matthew, up to this point in the story, few people have shown such faith, and many have doubted Jesus' teaching. Here, for example, Jewish officials in Jerusalem not only mistrust Jesus but also work to discredit him [v.15].

The exaggerated politeness with which Matthew describes the question from the Pharisees' flunkies makes them sound like bad actors: "Surely you, teacher, will tell the truth at all cost" [vv.16–17]. Matthew says that, despite this condescending bit of posturing, Jesus used the occasion to continue to teach. We hear that he dismissed their playacting, then got to the point [v.18]. Matthew assumes the reader realizes that the Jewish people weren't happy to pay a tax to their foreign occupiers, and that they resented even the reminder of this imposition as it was symbolized by Caesar's face and motto on a coin. But the Jewish people had no power to resist Caesar's tax, so they had to pay it [vv.19–21a].

However, the people had freely entered into a relationship with God: "I'm your God; you will have no others" (see Ex.20:2–3). This relationship frees God's people from turning to anyone else for their deepest needs. Jesus' teaching, as Matthew presents it, insists that, if you're a partner in this relationship—the Covenant—you should act out your commitment to it by giving God your complete trust. You should put yourself in God's hands [v.21b]. There's nothing more to say [v.22].

## ANOTHER TRAP, ANOTHER LESSON [MT.22:23–33]

*23 Later, Sadducees—those who maintained there was no resurrection—came up to him in the Temple to question him. 24 "Teacher, Moses said, 'If a man dies childless, his brother should take his wife and raise children with her' [Dt.25:5–6]. 25 Now, the first of seven brothers marries, dies childless, and leaves his wife to his brother. 26 Then the second dies, then the third, and so on to the seventh. 27 Then the woman dies. 28 In 'the resurrection,' whose wife will she be, if she was married to all?" 29 Jesus said, "You're confused because you know neither scripture nor God's power. 30 There's no marrying for the resurrected. In heaven we're like angels. 31 Haven't you read what God said [in scripture] about the resurrection of the dead? 32 'I am the God of Abraham, the God of Isaac, the God of Jacob' [Ex.3:6]. Well, he isn't God of the dead, but of the living!" 33 The crowds who heard this were dazzled by his teaching.*

Matthew has described Jesus' visit to the Temple (see 21:23) as a succession of challenges from influential Jewish groups. Here, some Sadducees, a group supporting priestly reform, try to trip Jesus up [v.23]. On the surface, their question seems both sensible and pious. They want to know how a Jew can live life forever and also live according to the Law that spells out the proper response to the Covenant [vv.24–28]. Matthew tells us Jesus said their question revealed ignorance about matters that devout students of the Law should understand [v.29].

We hear that their ignorance flowed from false assumptions. First, because they could see God's creation of human life unfolding here on earth, they assumed they understood God's creative plan. Matthew says Jesus corrected this assumption by saying those resurrected from the dead would be "like angels" [v.30]. Some readers might wish the dialogue included the question, "Teacher, how do you know that?" But the point here is not that Jesus knows something the Sadducees don't. The fact that they can't possibly be certain about the truth of their assertion is the lesson Jesus wants them to learn. Second, although they supposedly pored over scripture, they seemed not to recognize the God described there—a God who creates and sustains life; a God whose promises to care for Abraham and all his children were still alive and taking effect [vv.31–32].

From Matthew's description of the crowd's response we can guess either that they were excited by Jesus' clear profession of faith in God's everlasting care, or that they were surprised by the besting of the Sadducees—or both [v.33].

## ONE MORE CONFRONTATION;
## TWO MORE LESSONS [MT.22:34–46]

*³⁴ When the Pharisees heard he'd silenced the Sadducees, they came back to the Temple. ³⁵ A legal scholar among them asked Jesus a wily question: ³⁶ "Teacher, which is the great commandment of the Law?" ³⁷ "'You shall love the Lord, your God, with all your heart, with all your soul, and with all your mind' [Dt.6:5]," said Jesus. ³⁸ "This is the great and first commandment. ³⁹ The second is like it: 'Love your neighbor as yourself' [Lv.19:18]. ⁴⁰ These two sum up the Law, and the prophets." ⁴¹ Jesus then asked the Pharisees a question: ⁴² "What about 'the Christ'? Whose son is he?" "The son of David," they said. ⁴³ "Wasn't David inspired by the Spirit to call him 'Lord' [Ps.110:1]: ⁴⁴ 'The Lord said to my Lord, "Sit at my right as I put your enemies under your foot."' ⁴⁵ So, if David calls him 'Lord,' how can he be his son?" ⁴⁶ No one answered. And, from that day, they asked no more questions.*

The Pharisees here return to challenge Jesus' teaching [v.34]—asking a simple question, complicated by its range of possible answers [vv.35–36]. But Matthew tells us that Jesus simply reminded his listeners of verses from the Book of Deuteronomy, which all devout Jews pray several times a day to remind themselves of the essence of the Covenant [vv.37–38]. We hear Jesus add that the Covenant also requires us to care for our neighbor as God cares for us [v.39]. Those commands sum up the whole Covenant [v.40].

The question Matthew says Jesus put to the Pharisees about the identity of "the Christ"—a title derived from the Greek, meaning

God's "Anointed One" — is aimed at discovering how the Pharisees think God intends to fulfill the Covenant. Their answer suggests they thought God would fulfill his promise to care for them by anointing another king from the line of David — a descendant, or "son," who might return Israel to its ancient glory [vv.41–42]. But Matthew says Jesus told them to notice that scripture describes David expressing a much greater hope. He pictures David proclaiming the first words of Psalm 110 [vv.43–44]. Then Jesus asks them how the "Lord" whom God invites to sit at his right — and to whom the Lord, God, promises to give victory over all enemies — could be merely a descendant or son of David [v.45].

Matthew ends the scene with silence. We can picture the Pharisees thinking, "Wouldn't it be wonderful if God were to come personally to our aid," or thinking, "That's impossible!" Whatever the Pharisees may have thought, Matthew tells us they sought no more answers [v.46].

# TWENTY-THREE
## The Price of Lessons Not Learned

### JESUS WARNS AGAINST BAD EXAMPLE [MT.23:1–12]

*¹ Still in the Temple, Jesus turned to address his disciples and the people there: ² "Scribes and Pharisees have taken Moses' seat. ³ Follow their instructions, but not their example. ⁴ They put together heavy burdens for others' backs, but lift not a finger to help. ⁵ All their works are for show—such as enlarged phylacteries and lengthened tassels. ⁶ They love high places at banquets and the first seats in synagogues. ⁷ They love respectful greetings at the market, and to be called, 'Rabbi.' ⁸ Call none of you 'Rabbi.' You have one 'Teacher.' You're all 'siblings.' ⁹ Don't call anyone 'Father.' You have one Father in heaven. ¹⁰ Nor should you call anyone 'Master.' You have one Master, the Christ. ¹¹ The greatest among you will be your servant. ¹² Those who make themselves lofty will be humbled. Those who make light of themselves will be exalted."*

—⟋⟍⟋⟍—

With the Pharisees no longer asking questions (see 22:46), Matthew says Jesus turned to speak to his disciples and the remaining crowd [v.1], telling them, first, to respect the scholarship of teachers who, like Moses, interpret the Law. But we hear Jesus add that, though scribes and Pharisees could cite scripture accurately, they couldn't be trusted to interpret it properly [vv.2–3]. For instance, Matthew

121

describes some Jewish officials interpreting Sabbath rules so strictly they forgot the Sabbath's purpose (see 12:1–12); and we've heard that some officials made such a fetish of legalisms they failed to take the Law to heart (see 15:1–9). Here Matthew shows us Jesus accusing them of turning the Law into a burden [v.4] and being anxious to make their pious practices look more pious than the devotion of others [vv.5–7].

According to Matthew, Jesus wanted his disciples to behave differently—to notice they were all children of the same God. Children have to learn, of course, but Jesus says God's children won't need any teacher other than him [v.8]. Neither will they need a father other than God [v.9]; nor will they need a leader other than the one chosen and anointed for them by God [v.10]. We hear Jesus say that greatness—and that would include great piety—lies in noticing the needs of others and responding to them [v.11]. This is like God's greatness—the greatness of the God who promises eternal care for our needs. Those who puff themselves up grandly, even in displays of piety, will eventually deflate. But, as Jesus taught earlier [see 5:3], those who recognize their lowliness can let themselves be lifted up and cared for by God [v.12].

## A LAMENT ABOUT BAD TEACHING [MT.23:13–22]

*13 In the Temple, Jesus continued to speak to his disciples and the crowd. "Woe to you, scribes and Pharisees. Imposters! You bar the kingdom of heaven. You don't enter, and you keep others from entering! [14 Commentators say this line about stealing from widows is a late addition.] 15 Woe to you, scribes and Pharisees. Imposters! You travel sea and land for one convert, but make that one twice more eager than you to be a child of false worship. 16 Woe to you, blind guides. You say, 'Don't swear by the Temple, but by the Temple's gold.' 17 Blind and dim-witted! What's greater: Temple gold, or the Temple that sanctifies it? 18 You say, 'Don't swear by the altar, but by the gift on the altar.' 19 You're blind! What's greater: the gift, or the altar that makes it sacred? 20 An oath sworn 'By the altar!' includes everything on it. 21 Swearing 'By the Temple!' is a pledge by the Temple and by him who dwells there.* [22] *Swearing, 'By heaven!' swears by God's throne and by the God who sits there!"*

Here Matthew begins to describe an outburst of concern that continues below. Although the description lists numerous examples of gross obtuseness, it isn't the ravings of a teacher who's lost patience with ignorant students. It's an instruction on how to notice and avoid the seductive delusion that makes certain teachings so attractive—and so deadly. We may picture the now-silenced scribes and Pharisees still lurking in the crowd (see 22:46–23:1), but this lesson is a strong warning for anyone attracted to the opposite of the Good News of repentance.

Jesus is described complaining that some teach others that they can build the kingdom of heaven by carefully observing religious rules and rituals. This busy self-righteousness is not the way to the kingdom of heaven [v.13]. He also says that, when others are encouraged to indulge in pious self-regard, they'll find ways to double that haughty indulgence. Self-satisfaction, says Jesus, is the ultimate false worship—worship that will lead nowhere but to Gehenna, a place where everyone's ablaze with all-consuming regret [v.15]. Some teachers also encourage a self-consciously false reverence for God. They say, "Don't even mention his name!" They then concoct elaborate phrases to make themselves sound wise. This misleads God's children, who've been commanded by their Father to look to him for wisdom [vv.16–20].

Matthew says Jesus emphasized the freedom of God's children to appeal to their Father by reminding his audience that all needs are brought directly to God—not to the Temple, nor the heavens, nor to a throne [vv.21–22]. Though this is a lament, it's also a lesson in the Good News.

## THE LAMENT CONTINUES [MT.23:23–39]

²³ *"Woe to you, scribes and Pharisees. Hypocrites! You offer God ten percent of mint, dill, and cumin, but forget the Law's essence: justice, mercy, and faith. Do both! ²⁴ You're blind guides. You filter out a gnat, but swallow a camel. ²⁵ Woe to you, scribes and Pharisees. Hypocrites! You scrub the outside of cup and bowl, but let your insides remain full of greed and self-indulgence. ²⁶ Blind Pharisee! Scour the inside first! Then clean the surface. ²⁷ Woe to you, scribes and Pharisees. You're like whitewashed graves—perfect outside, but inside, piled with dead bones and all other foulness. ²⁸ You appear righteous to others, but within, you're full of deceit and wickedness. ²⁹ Woe to you, scribes and Pharisees. Hypocrites! You build tombs for the prophets and memorials to the righteous. ³⁰ You say, 'If we'd lived in our ancestors' day, we would not have helped them shed the prophets' blood.' ³¹ Your words reveal that you're descended from the prophets' assassins! ³² You complete the work of your ancestors! ³³ Snakes! Vipers' spawn! How can you avoid the blaze of Gehenna's eternal regret? ³⁴ Watch: I send prophets, sages, and scribes whom you'll kill, crucify, beat, and exile. ³⁵ On you is all the blood shed by all the righteous—from Abel, to Zechariah (killed in the Temple! [2 Chr.24:22]). ³⁶ O yes, indeed, I say this is the fate facing this generation. ³⁷ Jerusalem, Jerusalem, you killed the prophets and stoned God's messengers. I so wanted to gather your children together, as a hen gathers her brood, but you weren't willing. ³⁸ Look! Your house is abandoned. ³⁹ You won't see me until you say, 'Blessed is he who comes in the Lord's name.'"*

Matthew's description of Jesus' passionate instruction continues with examples of self-righteousness. We fuss about offerings, but forget they're intended to remind us that all is from God—especially the gifts of mercy, faith, and justice [v.23]. How foolish that fussiness looks [v.24]. We concentrate on good appearances, and ignore our ingrained greediness [v.25]. How backward [v.26]! We know tombs hide foulness, and we know the human heart is murky with conflicting desires [v.27]. How hard we work to pretend that isn't so [v.28]. We imagine ourselves as better than others [vv.29–30]; how unpleasant to see we're just like them [v.31]; how horrifying to think we're much worse [v.32]; and how disastrous it will be if we don't face this truth [v.33]. Whenever we hear followers of Jesus proclaiming repentance, we should recall that many before us resisted this message; and we should be shocked to find ourselves in such lethal company [vv.34–35]. Yes, that includes us [v.36]. Matthew portrays Jesus wanting to teach the inhabitants of Jerusalem — that is, all who've been invited into God's Covenant — to turn to God [v.37]. All have been chosen to be the abode of God; but we choose to live by ourselves, left in our own company [v.38]. But even now we could turn to Jesus as the one sent by God (see Ps.118:26) with Good News for those who need repentance [v.39]. What a blessing it would be to see ourselves as being spiritually poor — in need of the riches only God can give (see 5:3).

# TWENTY-FOUR
## Learning More about Repentance

### REPENTANCE TAKES A LIFETIME [MT.24:1–14]

¹ *As Jesus was leaving the Temple, his disciples pointed out its beauty.* ² *"All this?" he asked. "O yes, indeed, I say none of these stones will stay standing."* ³ *Later, on Mt. Olives, they asked, "What will be the sign of your coming—of the end?"* ⁴ *"Don't let others deceive you," said Jesus.* ⁵ *"Many will come in my name saying, 'I'm the Christ,' tricking many.* ⁶ *You'll hear of wars and threats of war. Don't worry. They'll come. It's not the end.* ⁷ *Nations will fight, kingdom against kingdom. There will be famines and earthquakes.* ⁸ *This is but the beginning of the birth struggle.* ⁹ *They'll persecute and kill you. Every nation will hate you because of my name.* ¹⁰ *Many will stumble and lose faith, betraying and hating one another.* ¹¹ *There will be many phony prophets, and they'll convince many.* ¹² *Because more and more will disregard the Law, many will become cold to love.* ¹³ *But those who are patient will find salvation.* ¹⁴ *The Good News of the kingdom will be proclaimed to all nations. Then the end will come."*

———∞∞∞———

Matthew says the disciples' awe of the Temple prompted Jesus to note it would one day fall [vv.1–2]. Previously, Matthew said Jesus assured them he would reappear when God's plan was fulfilled (see 10:23; 13:41; 16:27). Now they want to know what will signal the end—the fulfillment [v.3]. But Jesus tells them not to look for signs [vv.4–5]. People will continue to argue and fight as unpredictably as the rain falls and the earth shakes [vv.6–7] because humanity is still grappling with God's offer of love and care, and God's plan of creation is still in its early stage of unfolding [v.8].

Then we hear again about the strong resistance the disciples will meet (see 10:17ff.). When they proclaim people's need for God's care, many will feel insulted and will react violently [v.9]. Even some who once trusted in God's care will become prideful and unloving [v.10]. Any message that promotes self-confidence will be much more attractive than placing confidence in God [v.11]. If the Covenant of love is ignored, loving God and loving one another will seem pointless [v.12].

Although this sounds grim, we hear Jesus tell his disciples not to panic. It takes time to let go of anxiously fretting about oneself and turn, instead, to God for help. Life is a long process of learning that repentance leads to salvation, healing, and freedom from all distress [v.13]. Matthew says Jesus then told the disciples that the "end" would come only after people everywhere had heard the Good News that, if they repented, they would be on the way to the kingdom of heaven [v.14].

## REPENTANCE AND FAITHFULNESS WILL BE NECESSARY RIGHT TO THE END [MT.24:15–28]

[15] *Sitting on Mt. Olives with his disciples, Jesus continued to speak of "the end." "You'll see the 'abomination of desolation' standing in the Temple as Daniel described. (Let the reader take note [of Dn.9:27].)* [16] *Then those in Judea should flee to the mountains.* [17] *If you're on the roof, don't stop on the way down to take things from the house.* [18] *If you're in the field, don't run home for your cloak.* [19] *Alas for those pregnant or nursing at that time.* [20] *Hope the time for fleeing isn't in winter or on a Sabbath.* [21] *The distress at that time will be deep—never seen before, and never to recur.* [22] *If those days weren't cut short, no one would survive. But, for the Chosen, they'll be made brief.* [23] *If someone tells you, 'Here's the Christ!' or, 'No, over here!' don't believe them.* [24] *Phony Christs and prophets*

*will show up with signs and wonders to deceive, if possible, even the Chosen.* $^{25}$ *See? I've told you ahead of time.* $^{26}$ *So, if they say, 'He's in the desert,' don't go; or, 'He's in the pantry,' don't believe it.* $^{27}$ *Just as lightning in the east is seen all the way to the west, so the Son of Man will appear.* $^{28}$ *Where a corpse is, there will vultures gather.*

Matthew tells us Jesus associated "the end" with a rejection of the Covenant [v.15]. He says the disciples were reminded that the children of God once rejected God in favor of a foreign king (see Dn.9:27; 11:21–31), and he says they were told to flee from this sort of choice as far and as quickly as possible [v.16]. No possessions, not even clothes, should delay this flight [vv.17–18]. If people are hindered by a physical condition or need, or if weather or religious custom slows them down, they may find fleeing difficult, but they should flee [vv.19–20]. (We needn't associate this flight from danger with any particular historical event. The danger is posed not by particular individuals or circumstances but by selfishness in the heart.) There never was, nor ever will be, a worse fate, or "end," than choosing to be ruled by human ambitions [v.21]. And yet the impulse to satisfy our selfish cravings is potent. Given enough time, the impulse might overpower even those who've chosen to let God care for their needs [v.22].

We hear Jesus tell the disciples not to be seduced by those who say they've found a messiah [v.23]. Yes, anyone can fall prey to the persuasive power of a false message [v.24]. So remember this warning [v.25]. Jesus won't hide anywhere or appear secretly [v.26]. When he fulfills his promise to return (see 16:27), his arrival will be as obvious as lightning [v.27]. The appearance of Jesus—the Son of Man bringing the kingdom to all who've sought it—will be as obvious as buzzards circling a dead body [v.28]. It will be that clear.

## THE TEACHINGS OF JESUS, THE SON OF MAN,
## WILL PROVE TRUE [MT.24:29–35]

[29] *Jesus was still speaking of "the end" as he sat with his disciples on Mt. Olives. "After that troubled time, the sun will be dark, the moon won't shine, stars will fall, and all heavenly powers will crumble.* [30] *Then the sign of the Son of Man will appear. The tribes of the earth will repent when they see the Son of Man coming on heaven's clouds with power and great glory.* [31] *He'll send his angels to gather the Chosen with a trumpet blast from the four winds, from end to end of heaven.* [32] *Apply a lesson from the fig tree: when its branches become supple and begin to leaf, you know summer's near.* [33] *So, when you see these things, know the Son of Man is at the door.* [34] *O yes, indeed, I say this generation won't pass away until all this happens.* [35] *Heaven and earth will pass away. My words won't pass away."*

———⟨ɷɷɷ⟩———

Matthew's been portraying Jesus' description of "the end" with images used by the author of the Book of Daniel. Here [v.29], there are images from other prophetic books of scripture. Jesus' instruction is therefore a reminder of what hearers of scripture have already been taught: though all we see will fail, God's Covenant will prevail. With another echo from the Book of Daniel (see Dn.7:13), Jesus' words assure the disciples that he himself will be the evidence of God's power and glory—evidence so clear that all who take it in will be moved, at last, to repent [v.30]. There's no need to worry about missing this great moment. Just as the king in the parable went to great lengths to fill his feast (see 22:9–10), Jesus will send angels everywhere to assemble all who accepted God's invitation to be his Chosen Ones [v.31].

Then we hear Jesus encouraging his disciples to be as sensible about the signs of God's work as they are about the signs of the seasons [v.32]. Each year, we expect the summer. We're sure it will come, even if winter is exceptionally long and cold. We can be just as sure the kinds of things described above (starting at 24:5) will unfold. Even though such events may unsettle and shock us, they will open the door to Jesus revealing that the Good News is indeed true [v.33]. As Matthew narrates this Gospel, he knows we've heard of the resurrection. So, in a sense, the "generation" addressed by Jesus and by the evangelists has already witnessed his return in glory [v.34]. But the promise made by Jesus to return is not about a specific date. It's an assurance of a specific truth: all in this generation—this world, this creation—will surely see the things of earth fail. And, just as certainly, we'll see that Jesus' proclamation of God's kingdom (see 4:17) and his promise of its realization (see 5:6) will be fulfilled [v.35].

## SO, WAIT FOR JESUS' TEACHINGS TO PROVE TRUE [MT.24:36–51]

*[36] Jesus continued to speak about "the end" as he sat with his disciples on Mt. Olives. "No one knows the day or time [of the coming of the Son of Man]—not the angels; not the Son of Man; only the Father. [37] The coming of the Son of Man will be as it was in Noah's day. [38] Before the flood, they ate, drank, betrothed, married—right up to the time Noah boarded the ark. [39] They were heedless until the flood came. So, too, when the Son of Man comes. [40] Two men will be in a field, and one taken, the other left. [41] Two women milling flour; one taken, the other left. [42] So, watch! You don't know the day your Lord is coming. [43] If a householder knew when a thief was coming, he'd be awake to stop the break-in. [44] That's the reason for being ready—you don't know when the Son of Man will come. [45] Who's the wise, trusty slave asked by the master to feed and pay the others on time? [46] Happy the slave whom the master finds doing the task properly. [47] O yes, indeed, I tell you he'll put that one in charge of everything he owns! [48] But suppose a wicked servant says, 'My master delays his coming.' [49] Suppose he beats his fellow slaves, and eats and drinks with drunks. [50] That slave's master will come at an unexpected day and hour. [51] He'll cut him off and put him with hypocrites—with much grimacing and tears."*

———✦✦✦———

Matthew says Jesus told the disciples to leave the scheduling of creation's completion to the Father [v.36]. However, ignorance about the timing of God's plan shouldn't keep us from watching it unfold and looking forward to Jesus' return to share his glory—unless we want to ignore God, as did the people in the story of the flood [vv.37–39]. We don't have to stop life's ordinary activities in order to be attentive to God, but we should take care not to let daily life consume us. Otherwise, we'll find ourselves protesting, "But I can't be taken now; I have work to complete" [vv.40–41]. Let yourself be distracted by God's work, not yours. For example, we hear Jesus ask his disciples to imagine how a homeowner, warned of a break-in, would watch for any sign of an intruder. That's the sort of mindfulness we should practice [vv.42–44].

Another example of watchfulness describes servants left to run the household in the master's absence. Although Matthew portrays Jesus asking the disciples' opinion [v.45], Jesus' opinion is clear from the description of the servants' responses. One shares the master's concerns and is rewarded for that trustworthiness by being made a partner in the estate [vv.46–47]. The other servant doesn't think his master truly cares about the household. So he doesn't care for it either—only for himself [vv.48–49]. When the master returns suddenly, he'll accept the slave for what he is, a deceiver, and he'll banish him to the company of frauds. Once there, the faker will grind his teeth and weep with frustration over his foolish choice [vv.50–51].

# TWENTY-FIVE

## Repentance—Accepting the Covenant—Will Transform You

DO YOU TAKE THE COVENANT SERIOUSLY? [MT.25:1–13]

*¹ Jesus continued teaching his disciples on Mt. Olives. "The kingdom of heaven is like ten maidens who take oil lamps and go to meet a bridegroom. ² Five were thoughtless. Five were thoughtful. ³ The thoughtless didn't bring oil along with their lamps. ⁴ The thoughtful brought oil flasks as well as lamps. ⁵ When there was a delay in the bridegroom's arrival, they all became sleepy. ⁶ At midnight came the cry, 'Look! The bridegroom! Go meet him!' ⁷ All the maidens awoke and trimmed their lamps. ⁸ But the thoughtless said to the provident, 'Share your oil. Our lamps are going out.' ⁹ 'There's not enough for us all,' the others said. 'Go to the oil merchant and buy some.' ¹⁰ As they left, the bridegroom came, entered the wedding feast with the maidens who were prepared, and shut the door. ¹¹ Later, the other maidens came back and said, 'Lord, Lord, open up for us.' ¹² 'O yes, indeed,' he answered, 'I tell you I don't know you.' ¹³ So, keep watching, because you don't know the day or hour."*

————

This parable continues the above lessons in watchfulness, but also stresses the relationship—the Covenant—that creates our expectation of Jesus' return. In this story of a wedding party [v.1], Matthew

133

reports Jesus saying that some attendants took seriously their role as members of a wedding. Others didn't give it much thought [v.2]. Anyone who's been involved in a wedding knows weddings are complicated enough without worrying about the attendants. In this story, some women who were asked to welcome a bride to her new home with a parade of lights weren't prepared to fulfill their role [v.3]. Others, apparently sharing the groom's desire to give the bride a joyous reception, made special plans to do so [v.4].

Those who accept the role of groomsman or bridesmaid know they'll have to adjust their schedules to help a bride or groom. Matthew shows us that the attentive women in the parable were prepared to adjust to the groom's delay, but the other women not only were unready, but also expected others to share in their carelessness [vv.5–8]—a choice the prepared women didn't want to make [v.9]. We hear that the women who took the groom's invitation seriously made it possible for the feast to begin [v.10], and that the groom didn't recognize the tardy attendants because they were obviously not the women he'd thought they were: they hadn't taken a serious interest in his plans [vv.11–12]. So if you're interested in God's plan—his plan to bring us, his children, to his kingdom—you'll take the plan seriously and will keep watching for it to come to fruition [v.13].

## IS THE COVENANT A GOOD DEAL? [MT.25:14–30]

*14 As he sat with his disciples on Mt. Olives, Jesus said more about the kingdom. "It's like a man entrusting money to servants before going on a journey. 15 He gave one five talents; a second, two; a third, one—as suited their skills—and left. 16 The one with five talents put them to work and made five more. 17 And the second, with two talents, made two more. 18 But the fellow with one dug a hole and buried his master's money. 19 A long time passes, then the master returns to settle accounts with his servants. 20 The one given five came up and said, 'Lord, you gave me five; here's five more.' 21 'Well done, good, faithful servant,' he said. 'You were trusty in this small thing, so I'll put you in charge of much more. Enter into the joy of your master.' 22 Then the one given two said, 'Lord, you gave me* two, and I earned two more.' [23] 'Well done, good and faithful servant,' he said. 'You were trusty in small things, so I'll put you in charge of much more. Enter your master's joy.' [24] Then the fellow given one said, 'Lord, I knew you were tough—reaping where you didn't sow; harvesting what you didn't plant. [25] I was afraid. I hid the money in the ground. See, you have back what's yours.' [26] 'Wicked and lazy slave,' he said. 'You knew I reap where I don't sow, harvest what I don't plant. [27] You should've put the money with bankers so that, on my return, I'd get interest. [28] Take his talent. Give it to the one with ten. [29] Those who have will get more—to overflowing. Those who have not will lose all. [30] Throw this useless slave into the dark, where tears run and teeth grind.'"

———◦◦◦———

The simple and remarkable point of this story is that God wants to make his kingdom flourish by giving us full shares in it. The story says a property owner, who is intent on seeing his money earn a profit, makes it possible for his servants to follow his example by loaning them talents [vv.14–15]. (A talent was a large monetary unit. There's no play on the modern meaning of the word.) Two servants enjoy imitating the master [vv.16–17]. One other refuses to do so [v.18]. The master is so delighted by the attitude of the first servants that he makes them partners in his business [vv.19–23]. Though the third servant has some business skill (see v.15) and knows his master's wishes, he's reluctant to accept the opportunity to imitate him [vv.24–25]. The master is shocked that this servant has refused such an easy chance to work with him [vv.26–27]. Nonetheless, he allows him to go his own way—a way that leads to great regret [vv.28, 30]. Matthew also describes the master making the point that, if you keep investing in a good business, you'll make more and more money, but if you hoard your money and invest in nothing, your funds will dry up [v.29]. What Good News to hear that we're invited to be full partners with God in the kingdom. Why would anyone resist this deal—this Covenant?

## THE COVENANT AFFECTS ALL YOU DO [MT.25:31–46]

*[31] Jesus then talked about entering the kingdom. "When the Son of Man comes with his angels in glory, he'll sit on his throne of glory. [32] All nations will be assembled before him, and he'll divide them as a shepherd divides sheep from goats. [33] He'll put sheep to the right, goats to the left. [34] To those on the right, he'll say, 'Come, blessed by my Father. Inherit the kingdom prepared for you from the world's beginning. [35] For I was hungry, and you fed me; thirsty, you gave me a drink; a stranger, you invited me in. [36] I was naked, you clothed me; sick, you gave me care; imprisoned, you visited me.' [37] The righteous will say, 'Lord, when did we see you hungry and feed you, thirsty and give you drink? [38] When did we see you a stranger and invite you in, or naked and clothe you? [39] When did we come to you in sickness or in prison?' [40] 'O yes, indeed,' he'll say, 'I tell you, if you did it for the least of mine, you did it for me.' [41] Then he'll say to those on his left, 'Leave me, accursed, for the eternal fire made for the Deceiver and those who carry his message. [42] I hungered, you didn't feed me; thirsted, you gave me no drink. [43] You didn't take me in, a stranger; you didn't clothe my nakedness, or care for me, sick or imprisoned.' [44] They'll say, 'When, Lord, did we see you hungry, thirsty, an outsider, sick, or in prison and not care for you?' [45] 'O yes, indeed,' he'll say, 'I tell you what you didn't do for the least you didn't do for me.' [46] They'll go off to eternal regret; the righteous, to eternal life."*

Matthew says Jesus assured his disciples that, after everyone had heard the Good News (see 24:14), their reaction to it would be as clear to God as is the difference between a sheep and a goat to a shepherd [vv.31–33]. The righteous are righteous because they've made the right choice of turning to God for their needs—that is, repented. They're so accustomed to their choice that they scarcely notice how their neediness allows them to be moved by other people's needs [vv.34–39]. The Son of Man will remind them that, when they began to believe in God's care for them, they also began to see the needs of the rest of God's children [v.40]. But those who never feel it's necessary to turn away from their selfishness will see self-interest as natural. They won't notice others' needs because they'll have taught themselves to care only for themselves [vv.41–45].

The first part of the last line of the Greek text here can be translated, "They'll go off to eternal punishment." But the selfish aren't penalized by some outside force. They're allowed to damn themselves to eternal self-absorption. The right—or righteous—choice is to accept the gift of eternal life [v.46].

# TWENTY-SIX

## Passover, and the Rejection of Jesus

EXAMPLES OF ACCEPTING AND REJECTING
THE GOOD NEWS [MT.26:1–16]

*¹ When Jesus finished speaking about "the end," he told the disciples something else. ² "In two days, it's Passover, and the Son of Man will be handed over to crucifixion." ³ Meanwhile, the chief priests and elders had gathered in the courtyard of Caiaphas, the high priest. ⁴ They plotted to entrap Jesus and put him to death. ⁵ "But not during the Feast," they said. "The people could riot." ⁶ Later, at Bethany [see 21:17], Jesus was dining at the house of Simon, "the Leper." ⁷ A woman came up to him carrying, in alabaster, rich oil that she trickled on his head. ⁸ The disciples, upset by the sight, were saying, "Such waste! ⁹ That could have been sold for a great price, and the money given to the poor." ¹⁰ Jesus was aware of this and said, "Why belittle the woman? She's done me a good deed. ¹¹ You always have the poor; you don't always have me. ¹² This woman poured oil on me to prepare me for burial. ¹³ O yes, indeed, I tell you, wherever in the world the Good News is proclaimed, what she's done for me will be recalled." ¹⁴ Then Judas Iscariot, one of the twelve, went to the chief priests. ¹⁵ "What will you give if I hand him over?" he asked. They gave thirty silver coins. ¹⁶ He started looking for the moment to hand him over.*

Matthew has described official resistance to Jesus (see, e.g., 12:14), and Jesus' intention to face death (see 16:21; 17:22–23). Here, in two brief statements, he describes Jesus telling his disciples the feast of Passover would be the moment when those who planned his death would hand him over to a Roman-sanctioned execution—that is, crucifixion [v.2], and he describes the leaders of the Jerusalem community actually making plans for Jesus' death—but not, if they could manage it, during the feast [vv.3–5].

Then Matthew suddenly places us at a meal at the home of someone Jesus may have healed from leprosy [v.6]. And, just as suddenly, a woman disciple approaches and gives Jesus a lavish gesture of respect [vv.6–7], prompting the disciples at the table to complain that the gesture was an expensive waste [vv.8–9]. Matthew portrays Jesus as certain she'd done something good [v.10]. Then he describes him explaining why she was right to do what she did: her good deed was a way to prepare him for burial; and preparing him for death was a more immediate need than the ongoing need to care for the poor [vv.11–12]. Matthew has presented her action not just as a display of affection and comfort, but also as a proper response to Jesus' news that he would soon face death. Unlike the other disciples, she seems to have accepted this news [v.13]. Judas, on the other hand, not only rejects Jesus' version of Good News, he initiates a plan designed to silence its proclamation. Ironically, the plan Matthew tells us Judas set in motion would actually help fulfill the Good News [vv.14–16].

## JESUS CELEBRATES PASSOVER WITH HIS DISCIPLES [MT.26:17–30]

*[17] On the first day of Unleavened Bread, the disciples asked, "Where should we prepare the Passover meal for you?" [18] "Go into the city to this man," he said. "Say, 'The Teacher says, "My time is near. I'm keeping Passover with my disciples at your house."'" [19] They did as Jesus told them and prepared the Passover meal. [20] In the evening, he reclined at table with the twelve. [21] As they ate, he said, "Ah, yes, indeed, I tell you one of you will betray me." [22] This*

*distressed them deeply. They were all saying, "It isn't me, is it, Lord?" ²³ He said, "The one who's put his hand into the same dish with me will betray me. ²⁴ The Son of Man goes just as was written. But woe to the one who hands him over; better not to have been born." ²⁵ Judas, the betrayer, said, "It isn't me, is it, Rabbi?" "You've said it," he answered. ²⁶ As they ate, Jesus took bread, gave praise, broke it, gave it to the disciples, and said, "Take, eat, this is my body." ²⁷ He took the cup, gave thanks, and gave it to them saying, "Drink from it, all of you. ²⁸ This is my blood of the Covenant. It will be shed for many to forgive sins. ²⁹ I tell you, now I won't drink wine until I drink it with you in my Father's kingdom." ³⁰ They sang a hymn, then left for Mt. Olives.*

As Matthew continues to describe Jesus' last days, his narration seems almost rushed (see above, 26:2–7). But Jesus isn't portrayed as harried: he'd made plans with someone who would understand his message [vv.17–18]; disciples prepared the memorial meal (see Ex.12:14–20; vv.19–20); and Jesus continued to teach. First, we hear that he wanted his disciples to accept the fact that, though they were close enough to him to share this communal meal, they weren't all true to him [v.23]. They couldn't believe this [vv.21–22], so Jesus reminded them that scripture describes just such personal animosity [v.24a]. Then, in an appeal to Judas to repent of his deadly plan, we hear Jesus say it will bring destruction on the perpetrator [v.24b]. When Judas asked for a plain answer, Jesus gave him one [v.25].

Judas isn't mentioned again in this scene, as the narrative moves quickly through the rest of the meal as if nothing much happened — except this: Jesus gave himself to his disciples. Matthew describes him doing this in the same way he'd fed the hungry (see 14:19; 15:36) — that is, he gave thanks and praise to his Father [vv.26–27]. In Matthew's account, Jesus' blood — his life — is spoken of as the very life and essence of the Covenant. For Jesus' life was consumed by only one thing: seeking to share God's life. He didn't cling to life as we know it. We hear that all who shared his choice, and repented of all other choices, would know forgiveness and divine life [v.28].

Jesus now looked forward to nothing else but sharing that life with those who, like him, sought it [v.29]. Matthew says that, to end this meal, all joined in singing praise [v.30].

## JESUS FEELS ABANDONED BY ALL
## BUT HIS FATHER [MT.26:31–46]

*[31] On Mt. Olives, Jesus says, "You'll fall away from me tonight. It's written: 'I'll strike the shepherd, and the flock will scatter' [see Zec.13:7]. [32] But after I'm raised, I'll go before you to Galilee." [33] Peter said, "Others may fall away, but I never will." [34] "O yes, indeed, I tell you, before a cock crows, you'll deny me three times." [35] "Even if it meant dying, I'd never deny you," said Peter. The others said the same. [36] At Gethsemane, "the Oil Press," Jesus said, "Sit here while I go and pray." [37] He invited along Peter and the sons of Zebedee, but was mournful and distressed. [38] "My soul is torn apart to the point of death," he said. "Stay and watch with me." [39] He moved off, fell on his face, and prayed, "Father, if possible, let this cup pass. But, not as I want—as you want." [40] Going to his disciples, he finds them asleep: "Peter, you couldn't watch one hour? [41] Watch, pray, or you'll give in to temptation. The Spirit's eager, but flesh is feeble." [42] He prayed again, "Father, if this can't happen lest I drink, your will be done." [43] He found them sleeping again, their eyes heavy with sleep. [44] He left, and prayed the same thing again. [45] Going back to them, he says, "Still sleeping? Look: this hour the Son of Man is handed to sinners. [46] Get up. Let's go. See? My betrayer is right here."*

Matthew continues to narrate Jesus' last hours succinctly. Though he just described Jesus and his disciples praising God with expressions of faith (see 26:30), Jesus is now portrayed asking his disciples to consider the possibility that, like people described in the Book of Zechariah, they will be faithless [v.31]. Then we hear him say that, despite their faithlessness, he will return to them [v.32]. Matthew says Peter refused to imagine he could be faithless [v.33], and Jesus left him with a warning [v.34] that would later become a lesson (see below, v.75). We hear that Peter, still unrepentant, clung to his idea of himself, and was joined in his blindness by all the others [v.35].

The scene shifts suddenly to the grounds of an oil press on Mt. Olives, where Jesus asked the disciples to pray [v.36]. Matthew says Jesus told his closest friends about his dread and his need for their support in turning to God in prayer [vv.37–38]—a prayer with a direct and simple request: "I *want* you to do as I desire, but I *ask* you to do what you desire" [v.39]. He then says Jesus again sought the support of his three friends, but found none [v.40]. Then we see that, even in the midst of deep distress, Jesus taught—here, telling his friends that, if they didn't seek the Spirit's help to turn to God, they'd be tempted to turn elsewhere [v.41]. Matthew says Jesus repeated his request to the Father [v.42], but failed—again—to find support from his friends [v.43]. We hear that Jesus petitioned his Father yet again [v.44], then, his dread apparently gone, he asked his disciples to notice that the fate he'd accepted from the Father was now standing in front of them [vv.45–46].

## JESUS IS ARRESTED; THE DISCIPLES FLEE [MT.26:47–56]

*[47] As Jesus spoke, Judas, one of the twelve, arrived with an armed crowd from the chief priests and elders of the people. [48] The betrayer had given them a sign: "I'll kiss the one you're to arrest." [49] He went right up to Jesus, said, "Joy to you, Rabbi," and kissed him. [50] "Friend," said Jesus, "do what you've come to do." They grabbed and arrested him. [51] One of those with Jesus drew a sword, swiped at the high priest's servant, and cut off his ear. [52] "Put back your sword," said Jesus. "Those who take up the sword will die by it. [53] Do you think I can't ask my Father to send more than twelve legions of angels? [54] But, then, how would we see how truly the scriptures described this?" [see 26:31]. [55] He said to the crowd, "Do you come with swords and clubs as if to arrest a criminal? I sat teaching every day in the Temple and you didn't arrest me. [56] But this all happens in order to reveal how fully the prophets' writings spoke true." Then all the disciples fled, leaving him alone.*

Matthew describes Jesus' arrest as one more lesson for the disciples, and he does so in the same bare-bones manner as the last few scenes (see 26:1–46). An armed contingent sent by officials in Jerusalem had arrived [v.47] while Jesus was still speaking of prayer (see 26:45–46). A prearranged signal of betrayal was performed with a display of respect [vv.48–49]. Jesus' use of the term "friend" may be seen either as a tribute to the irony of the situation, or as one last appeal to Judas to recognize a relationship he'd rejected. Matthew then tells us that, when it was clear there would be no resistance from Jesus, he was immediately taken into custody [v.50].

Next, we hear that one of the disciples refused to heed or follow Jesus' lead. If Jesus wouldn't resist, he'd do it for him [v.51]. The need for lessons never seems to end. So Jesus is once more portrayed reminding his disciples of the choice they must make. In this case, they could choose violence against others, or they could avoid that dead end [v.52]. We also hear Jesus asking them to imagine that God's power was working—unless they chose to suppose God couldn't rescue Jesus; or that Jesus had forgotten to ask the Father for what he needed [v.53]. Then we hear that, with gentle, almost comic irony, Jesus told them they'd never see how truly scripture had already described their fear if they kept pretending they were strong [v.54].

Matthew shows Jesus also teaching the crowd, asking them to note the difference between their treatment of him now and, earlier, in the Temple [v.55]. He draws a lesson for them, saying that these events, as well as scripture, were revealing God's way of working— a way of working that Matthew describes the disciples fleeing [v.56].

## JESUS IS REJECTED BY JERUSALEM'S OFFICIALS [MT.26:57–68]

*57 The arresting contingent took Jesus to Caiaphas, the high priest, where the scribes and elders had gathered. 58 Peter followed him at a distance, entered the high priest's courtyard, and sat with the servants to see what would happen.*

[59] *The chief priests and the official Council sought testimony for a death sentence.* [60] *They didn't find much, though there were many witnesses. Then two stood up:* [61] *"This one said, 'I can destroy God's Temple, and rebuild it in three days.'"* [62] *The high priest got up and said, "You say nothing to this testimony?"* [63] *Jesus said nothing. "I order you, under oath, to tell us: Are you the Messiah, the Son of God?"* [64] *"Your words," said Jesus. "I say, 'Now you'll see the Son of Man sitting at the Power's right, and coming on the clouds of heaven' [Dn.7:13; Ps.110:1]."* [65] *The high priest ripped his clothing and said, "Blasphemy! No more testimony; we've heard blasphemy!* [66] *What's your opinion?" They said, "Blasphemy deserves capital punishment."* [67] *They spat in his face. They beat and punched him.* [68] *They said, "Reveal to us, 'Anointed One,' who hit you!"*

Matthew depicts the Jerusalem authorities prepared for Jesus to be brought before them [v.57]. Peter is described as still unable to believe what he's been taught (see 16:22) as he waits in apparent bewilderment [v.58]. But the authorities are portrayed as certain. They seek an excuse to pronounce a death sentence [v.59]. Matthew describes the scene descending into farce. The plotting officials haven't arranged convincing perjury [v.60], so they give credence to an obvious distortion [v.61] as if it were Jesus' actual words (compare with 24:2). The high priest then pretends to be puzzled by Jesus' lack of defense [v.62], and demands an explanation of his claims [v.63]. Jesus ignores the implication that he's claimed a power he doesn't have, and says he believes God will fulfill the divine plan in a way that's like the description of it that's found in the Book of Daniel [v.64]. At that point, we see the high priest make a sanctimonious display of horror [v.65]. The stunning irony here is that, if the officials truly believed in the Covenant, they'd rejoice in Jesus' reminder that God was intent on fulfilling the Covenant: "The Lord said, 'Take your throne at my right hand!'" (Ps.110:1).

But Matthew describes the high priest as just the first of many officials who pretend that Jesus' profession of faith was a denial of faith. They profess to understand his words as a rejection of God so absolute that it deserves the penalty of death [v.66]. As Matthew depicts it, their behavior follows a simple logic: Jesus can be treated as an abomination [v.67], and the possibility that he might be God's Anointed One could be rejected as a joke [v.68].

### PETER REJECTS JESUS, THEN REPENTS [MT.26:69–75]

*69 Peter was still sitting in the courtyard. A maid came up to him and said, "You were with Jesus the Galilean." 70 He denied that in front of everyone: "I don't know what you're saying!" 71 He went out the gate, and another maid saw him. She said, "This one was with Jesus of Nazareth." 72 He again denied it and swore he didn't know him. 73 Later, bystanders came over and said, "Your accent shows you're one of them." 74 He completely rejected that and swore again, "I don't know the man." Right then, a cock crowed. 75 Peter remembered Jesus' words, "Before the cock crows, you'll deny me three times." He went away and wept bitterly.*

Matthew's narration of events after Judas' offer of betrayal (see 26:15)—from preparations for the Passover meal, through the meal itself, during the praying at the Olive Press, the arrest, and the phony trial—unfolded swiftly. But now it goes into painful detail describing Peter's inability to accept a situation that Jesus had tried to teach the disciples to see as inevitable (see 10:25; 16:21; 17:22–23; 20:18). Because Matthew mentions no outright threats against Peter, his description of the three refusals to tell the truth suggests a vehemence the situation doesn't actually call for. Could he be asking us to realize that, in a sense, Peter's denials are honest—that is, that Jesus isn't the man he thought he knew? He's told us that Jesus pleaded with Peter to reject the temptation to follow his own notions of security and achievement (see 16:23). Here, it's obvious that Peter still can't do that, despite Jesus' recent warning that Peter shouldn't trust his ideas about himself (see 26:34).

This description of Peter hammers home the reality that Matthew told us Jesus stressed: we panic when we think we've been abandoned by God (see 26:31, 54). Here, we see Peter trying to protect himself with lies because he apparently couldn't imagine any other way to save himself from trouble. We certainly don't see him imagining the possibility that God, who promises in the Covenant to care for us, might actually come to his aid. Then, says Matthew, Peter was surprised by a cock's crow into recognizing how thoroughly he had lied to himself and to Jesus. His tears suggest that he repented of those lies.

# TWENTY-SEVEN

## Accomplishing Jesus' Death

### JUDAS REGRETS HIS CHOICE [MT.27:1–10]

*¹ In the morning, the chief priests and elders considered how to put Jesus to death. ² They led him off, bound, and handed him over to Pilate, the Roman Governor. ³ When Judas, his betrayer, saw him condemned, he had regrets. He brought back the thirty pieces of silver to the elders and chief priests. ⁴ "I've sinned," he said, "betraying innocent blood." They said, "So? That's your concern." ⁵ He threw the silver into the Temple and he went off and hanged himself. ⁶ The chief priests picked up the money: "We can't put blood money in the treasury." ⁷ So they decided to buy a certain potter's field as a place to bury strangers. ⁸ That plot is therefore known, even today, as the Field of Blood. ⁹ The truth spoken by the prophet Jeremiah was then fully seen: "They took the thirty pieces—the amount offered by the Children of Israel. ¹⁰ It was given for a potter's field, as the Lord directed" [see, not Jer., but Zec.11:13].*

———⦿⦿⦿———

For the next several scenes in this Gospel, Jesus seems powerless. Others go about their business, using him as a pawn in what seems to them a larger game. As Matthew narrates it, the first order of business for the Jerusalem officials was to secure a death sentence from the Roman authorities [vv.1–2]. Judas' bit of business was to

149

try to undo his treachery. When he got no help from the religious officials who had conspired with him [vv.3–4], he apparently thought there was no one he could turn to, so he took his own life [v.5]. He's portrayed as able to regret what he did [v.3], but unwilling to seek forgiveness. Matthew lets us wonder why Judas' desire to find righteousness apparently didn't lead him to beg for it as a blessing (see 5:6).

Matthew then portrays Jerusalem's religious leaders dealing coolly and efficiently with the betrayal money. They hesitate to use it for Temple purposes [v.6], but not to spend it on what they consider a worthy project [v.7]. Nothing suggests they felt any compunction, even though the source of the money eventually became public knowledge [v.8].

The phrases Matthew attributes to Jeremiah are adapted from an extended image in the Book of Zechariah, which, at one point, pictures a fee of thirty silver pieces being flung into the Temple after it was begrudgingly paid by God's faithless people. One need not catch all the allusions contained in this passage to understand what appears to be Matthew's point: the relationship between God and his people has often broken down. But this relationship is created and directed by—and will be fulfilled by—the Lord [vv.9–10].

## ANOTHER PRETENSE AT JUSTICE [MT.27:11–26]

*[11] The Governor asked Jesus, "Are you King of the Jews?" "Your words," said Jesus. [12] To accusations from the chief priests and elders, Jesus said nothing. [13] "Don't you hear the testimony they bring against you?" said Pilate. [14] He said not a word. The Governor was perplexed. [15] It was a Festival custom for the Governor to release a prisoner at Passover chosen by the crowd. [16] One infamous prisoner was a man called Barabbas. [17] Pilate turned to the crowd: "Whom shall I free: Barabbas, or Jesus, the Anointed?" [18] (He realized the authorities had handed him over because of enviousness.) [19] As he sat in judgment, his wife sent word: "I've had a troubling dream. Do nothing with this just man." [20] The chief priests and elders told the crowd: "Ask for Barabbas—and for Jesus' death." [21] "Whom do you want me to release?" Pilate asked. "Barabbas," they said. [22] He*

said, *"What shall I do with Jesus, called the Anointed?" "Crucify him," they said.* [23] *"Why? What's he done wrong?" he asked. But they yelled louder, "Crucify him!"* [24] *Pilate saw he was producing nothing but mayhem. He washed his hands publicly and said: "I'm innocent of this man's blood. You look to it."* [25] *The crowd said, "Let his blood be on us and our children."* [26] *He then gave them Barabbas. He ordered Jesus scourged and crucified.*

Matthew begins this scene after Pilate's obviously been told by the Jerusalem officials that Jesus has been claiming allegiance to a kingdom other than Rome—an accusation Jesus won't discuss [v.11]. Matthew tells us that, when the officials repeated and expanded on their complaint, and Jesus continued to refuse to defend himself, Pilate didn't know how to proceed [vv.12–14]. But then he had a thought: he'd use the Passover feast, and a custom that seems to reflect the feast's celebration of freedom and salvation, to urge leniency [vv.15–17]. Matthew also tells us Pilate understood the officials' motive [v.18], and that his wife's misgivings about the trial were so strong that she intervened on Jesus' behalf [v.19].

According to Matthew, Pilate's attempt to guide the hearing was too tepid for the heat of an organized shouting match [vv.20–22]. His request for facts is hooted down by cries of blood lust [v.23]. Then Pilate performed a dumb show of personal probity—an offhand warning to an angry crowd that they were demanding something that was wrong [v.24]. We hear that, when the crowd pretended they could take responsibility for the sentencing themselves, Pilate made the convoluted decision that, since the crowd was content with injustice, he'd give them an official order for it [vv.25–26]. When those who recite the Apostles' Creed say they believe Jesus "suffered under Pontius Pilate," they recall that Jesus' murder was contrived and carried out by a legally sanctioned judicial system.

## THE OFFICIAL SENTENCE IS CARRIED OUT [MT.27:27–44]

*<sup>27</sup> Governor's troops took Jesus inside the fortress. A whole contingent assembled. <sup>28</sup> They stripped off his clothes and put a scarlet cloak on him. <sup>29</sup> They twisted thorny branches into a circlet and crowned him. They put a stick in his right hand. They knelt and guffawed, "Hail, King of the Jews." <sup>30</sup> They spat on him and smacked him on the head with the stick. <sup>31</sup> After the mockery, they removed the cloak, dressed him, and led him to crucifixion. <sup>32</sup> On the way, they met Simon, a Cyrenian, and forced him to carry the cross. <sup>33</sup> They reached Golgotha, that is, "Skull Place." <sup>34</sup> They offered bitter wine to kill his thirst, but he didn't want it. <sup>35</sup> They put him on the cross and divided his clothing by shares. <sup>36</sup> They then sat down to keep watch. <sup>37</sup> They'd hung the charge above his head: "This is Jesus, King of the Jews." <sup>38</sup> Capital criminals were crucified with him, one on each side. <sup>39</sup> Passersby taunted him and waggled their heads. <sup>40</sup> "If you can knock down the Temple and remake it in three days, save yourself." "If you're the son of God, come down from the cross." <sup>41</sup> The chief priests and elders also mocked him. <sup>42</sup> "The king of Israel saves others, not himself!" "If he can get down, we'll believe!" <sup>43</sup> "He trusted God, let God save him!" "He calls himself 'God's son'!" <sup>44</sup> The crucified criminals also made fun of him.*

Matthew uses a succinct, matter-of-fact style to describe events leading up to Jesus' arrest and first interrogation. Now, after lingering on the struggles of Peter, Judas, and Pilate to deal with unpleasant truths, Matthew's narrative again speeds up. His narrative sounds almost like a police report as he tells us how the occupying soldiers carried out their orders with efficient precision: breaking the prisoner [vv.27–31]; commandeering help [v.32]; arriving at the assigned place [v.33]; offering a potion (to hurt? to help?) [v.34]; taking care of the condemned's effects; setting a guard [vv.35–36]; posting an official accusation that Jesus had posed as a king [v.37]; and carrying out other crucifixions scheduled for that day [v.38].

Then Matthew tells us that groups as various as casual observers, religious authorities, and the two capital criminals felt free to judge Jesus as a fraud who'd been caught making outrageous promises that obviously couldn't be fulfilled: "If you know something greater than our great Temple, let's see you call upon this greatness and get help from it!" [vv.39–40]; "If you know God so well, let him save you from death!" [vv.41–43]. Matthew tells us that, as Jesus faces this desperate situation, his teaching about God's care for him seemed laughable to tough-minded realists such as the criminals who were executed with him [v.44].

## JESUS DIES [MT.27:45–56]

*⁴⁵ From noon until three, it was dark. ⁴⁶ Around three, Jesus cried loudly, "Eli, Eli, lema sabachthani"—that is, "My God, my God, why have you abandoned me?" [the beginning of Psalm 22]. ⁴⁷ Some bystanders, mishearing "Eli," said, "He's calling on Elijah." ⁴⁸ One of them rushed to soak a sponge in cheap wine, and offered it to him on a stick. ⁴⁹ Others said, "Wait! See if Elijah comes to save him!" ⁵⁰ Jesus again cried loudly, then gave up the spirit. ⁵¹ Imagine, the Temple curtain ripped in two, top to bottom. Earth shook; rocks split. ⁵² Tombs were opened. Many bodies of the saints who'd fallen asleep were raised. ⁵³ Released from their tombs, they entered the city after his resurrection and appeared to many. ⁵⁴ When the centurion and the guard watching Jesus saw the earthquake and other things, they were deeply frightened. They said, "Truly, this was God's Son." ⁵⁵ Viewing this from a distance were many women who'd followed Jesus from Galilee to care for him. ⁵⁶ Among them: Mary Magdalene; Mary, mother of James and Joseph; and the mother of Zebedee's sons.*

Matthew's been describing Jesus as powerless (see comments on 27:1–2). Here, he depicts him under a lowering sky, praying Psalm 22—a complaint about the apparent uselessness of turning to God, but also a profession of trust that, despite appearances, God will deliver the despised and afflicted [vv.45–46]. Some who heard Jesus' prayer supposedly heard it as a cry to Elijah for help [v.47]. Earlier, Matthew described Jesus saying that scripture's promise of a reappearance by Elijah to proclaim repentance and reconciliation (see Mal.3:23) had been fulfilled (see above, 11:14; 17:10–12). Now, he says that some bystanders, perhaps certain that Jesus would get no help from Elijah, offered the more tangible relief of wine. Others joked about the possibility of an Elijah sighting [vv.48–49]. Then, he says, Jesus prayed once more to the Father. Then he died [v.50].

For a believer, earthquakes and their damage—even to places of worship—are part of God's creative plan. Jesus taught his disciples to expect them and also to expect the eventual triumph of God's plan (see 24:29–31). Here, Matthew says that signs such as the torn Temple curtain, the shaking earth, and the raising of the dead [vv.51–53] provoked an astonished belief in the Gentile soldiers. They suddenly saw Jesus as God's Son, not as the outcast he appeared to be [v.54]. Matthew describes the women who followed Jesus as caring disciples who are attentive to the end [v.55]. By naming three women, Matthew reminds us this was no faceless group, but individual friends of Jesus, struggling to have faith in him [vv.55–56].

## JESUS IS BURIED [MT.27:57–66]

*⁵⁷ On the scene comes a rich man from Arimathea, Joseph, who was Jesus' disciple. ⁵⁸ He went to Pilate for Jesus' body. Pilate gave the order for the transfer. ⁵⁹ Joseph took the body and wrapped it in fresh linen. ⁶⁰ He placed it in a tomb he'd recently had cut for himself from rock. He rolled a large stone across the entrance and left. ⁶¹ Mary Magdalene and Mary, mother of James and Joseph, sat by the tomb. ⁶² The next day—the preparation day for the Sabbath—the chief priests and Pharisees went to Pilate. ⁶³ "Lord," they said, "we recall that, in life, that fake said, 'After three days, I'll rise.' ⁶⁴ So, put a guard at the grave for three days. Otherwise, his disciples will steal the body and tell everyone he's risen. That bit of trickery will be worse than all the others." ⁶⁵ Pilate said, "You've got Temple soldiers; you take care of it." ⁶⁶ They went to the tomb, sealed it, and set a guard.*

—⎯⎯⎯

This might not seem an appropriate moment for a touch of humor, but, after Jesus' strong warning to the disciples about the danger of riches (see above, 19:22ff.), the sudden appearance of a rich disciple who had enough influence to contact Pilate and ask for a favor is remarkable and slightly amusing. In Matthew's narration of this story, his money and influence made it possible to bury Jesus with care—even reverence [vv.57–60]. Once Matthew has described the rich man's work, he turns his focus to the silently attentive women disciples. They put into practice one of Jesus' most basic lessons: "Watch" (see, e.g., 24:42). Not sure what to expect, they sit and watch [v.61].

On the other hand, Matthew tells us the Jerusalem authorities established quite a different watch. He describes the women watching with patience and trust; he describes the Jewish authorities trusting no one. According to him, the authorities warned Pilate that, when Jesus professed confidence in the Father (see, e.g., 12:38–40), he was actually making remote plans for his disciples to conspire in a fraud [vv.62–63]. So they suggested a plan to abort this supposed conspiracy [v.64]—a plan Pilate leaves to them [v.65]. Then they went about the business of protecting themselves from fraud—another touch of humor [v.66].

# TWENTY-EIGHT

## Jesus Is Raised from the Dead; He Sends the Disciples to Proclaim This Good News

### RISEN FROM DEATH [MT.28:1–10]

*¹ After the Sabbath, as the first day of the week was dawning, Mary Magdalene and Mary, mother of James and Joseph, came to look at the tomb. ² Imagine, there was a large quake. An angel of the Lord descended from heaven, rolled away the stone, and sat there. ³ The angel seemed like lightning clothed in snow. ⁴ The guards shook with fear at the sight, and then appeared to be dead. ⁵ The angel's response was to say to the women, "Don't be afraid. I know you seek Jesus, who was crucified. ⁶ He's not here. He's raised—just as he said. Come, see where he was lying. ⁷ Go, quickly. Tell his disciples, 'He's raised from the dead and goes ahead to Galilee where you'll see him.' That's my message." ⁸ They left quickly, frightened, but giddy with joy. They ran to tell his disciples. ⁹ Then, imagine, Jesus met them: "Hello." They went up to touch his feet in homage. ¹⁰ "Don't be afraid," he said. "Tell my brothers to go to Galilee to see me there."*

———∞∞∞———

Matthew gives no reason for the visit of the two Marys to the tomb other than "to look" [v.1]. If we suppose they planned to mourn, we see them, instead, stunned (along with the guards) by an apparition of a dazzling heavenly messenger [vv.2–4] who knows their concern [v.5], but tells them they're looking in the wrong place for Jesus. This message shouldn't surprise them. As Jesus' disciples, they would have heard the assurance that Matthew says Jesus gave to the disciples that he expected to be raised (see, e.g., 17:22–23). So, of course the place to look for him wouldn't be a tomb [v.6]. Matthew tells us the messenger immediately sent them to remind the other disciples of Jesus' promise to meet them in Galilee (see 26:32) once he'd been raised from the dead [v.7].

Matthew describes the women as both unsettled and delighted to be carrying the first news of the resurrection [v.8]. It's easy to suppose their jumble of emotions spinning even more dizzily out of control in response to a greeting from Jesus. Matthew depicts them instinctively falling at Jesus' feet [v.9], but then he tells us Jesus wanted them free of fear as they brought the Good News to the others. "And don't forget," says Jesus, "to remind them of the promise to meet in Galilee after I'd been raised" [v.10]. Matthew doesn't portray the resurrection with great spectacle. In fact, it's not described at all. The only moment that can be pictured as spectacle is the appearance of an angel to announce that the resurrection had already taken place. Matthew focuses on one simple effect of the resurrection: the disciples are to meet with Jesus.

## DOUBTS ABOUT THE GOOD NEWS [MT.28:11–20]

*[11] As the women went off on their mission, some of the guard went into the city and told the chief priests what had happened. [12] The priests consulted with the elders, and they gave the soldiers plenty of silver. [13] They told them, "Say, 'His disciples came while we slept at night and took him.' [14] If the Governor hears of it, we'll mollify him and keep you out of it." [15] They took the silver and followed orders. Their story is still told among the Jews. [16] The eleven disciples went to the mountain in Galilee as Jesus had asked. [17] Seeing him, they did him homage, but some doubted. [18] Jesus went up to them: "All power in heaven and on earth is given to me. [19] So, go make disciples of all nations—baptizing them in the*

*name of the Father, and of the Son, and of the Holy Spirit.* [20] *Teach them to keep all I commanded you. Look, I am with you all days to the end of the age."*

With a few sentences, Matthew paints a picture of anxious collusion in a lie. He tells us it made more sense to the Jerusalem authorities to pay for this lie, rework it so that it would be acceptable to the Roman authority, and then spread it about in the Jewish community [vv.11–15] than to consider the possibility that Jesus' witness before them was proving true (see 26:64). But they weren't the only ones to doubt the possibility that Jesus had proclaimed the truth.

Matthew says Jesus' closest remaining disciples—his "brothers" (see 28:10)—traveled as they'd been told (see above, v.10) to a high place in Galilee [v.16]. A mountain site, not mentioned before (see 26:32), suggests a desire for privacy, but its choice isn't explained. Matthew says some of the eleven greeted Jesus, like the women in the previous scene (see above, v.9), with a gesture of worship. Some, however, are described as hesitant [v.17]. Matthew tells us Jesus went right up to his doubt-filled friends and sent them on a mission that the Father had empowered him to give them [v.18]. There's no word of rebuke. According to Matthew, both the worshipful and the doubtful were sent to do what Jesus had been doing. They were to proclaim repentance—a baptism—in the name of the Father (who offers the promise of divine life), in the name of the Son (whose dying and rising gives witness that the Father's offer is trustworthy), and in the name of the Spirit (who fulfills this promise by giving divine life to those who turn and ask for it) [v.19]. They were to proclaim the same lessons Jesus taught them [v.20a]. Though their mission might seem to be too much for their feeble convictions to complete, they could take heart from Jesus' promise to be with them always [v.20b].

# Index

# About the Author

**Paul J. McCarren**, SJ, works at Loyola Retreat House and at St. Ignatius Church, both in Maryland, while continuing to write Simple Guides to the Bible. A Jesuit priest, he has spent many years in both parish and campus ministry.